PLAY ACTIVITIES FOR THE RETARDED CHILD

BERNICE WELLS CARLSON
DAVID R. GINGLEND

Illustrated by Darrell K. Sweet

ABINGDON PRESS — NEW YORK • NASHVILLE

PLAY ACTIVITIES
FOR
THE
RETARDED CHILD

How to Help Him Grow and Learn Through Music,
Games, Handicraft, and Other Play Activities

PLAY ACTIVITIES FOR THE RETARDED CHILD

Copyright © 1961 by Abingdon Press

Library of Congress Catalog Card Number: 61-5554

"He's Got the Whole World in His Hands,"
p. 174; "Elephant Song," p. 169; "If You're
Happy and You Know It," p. 167; "Rig-a-jig-
jig," p. 183, "This Old Man," p. 171, ap-
peared in the pamphlet accompanying Folkway Records Album No. FC 7659, "Learn As
We Play," copyright © 1959 by Folkway
Records and Service Corp., 117 W. 46th St.,
New York, New York.

SET UP, PRINTED, AND BOUND BY THE
PARTHENON PRESS, AT NASHVILLE,
TENNESSEE, UNITED STATES OF AMERICA

To **Marta** and **Marian**
and the
Raritan Valley Unit
New Jersey Association for Retarded Children

PREFACE

THE MENTALLY RETARDED CHILD who, for centuries upon centuries, has been lost to society, is at last finding his place thanks largely to the National Association for Retarded Children, Incorporated, whose growth has alerted, and increasingly interested, the general public in the subject of retardation. Likewise, it has encouraged many more professional people to enter the related fields of work concerned with this problem, such as: medicine, psychology, education, social work, general research, and so on. NARC and its member units have worked for better legislation and have achieved it on a national level and in many states, protecting the rights of this special group of persons.

All kinds of people have retarded children: rich and poor, young and old, wise and foolish, healthy and weak, people of every nationality, every race. Retarded children themselves vary greatly. In any community we are likely to find retardates of all ages, with different temperaments, different physical abilities, and varying degrees of mental retardation. This book has been written to help train the young retarded child. By young, we mean a person young in mental years—an educable child who is young chronologically and a more severely retarded child who has a low mental age and almost any chronological age. In general, this book is written for use with children of six years mental age or younger. It is directed primarily to help parents working with a child, first in the home and later in play

7

or school groups. It can also be used to advantage by recreation leaders and teachers working with retarded children in private, public, or institutional schools or anyone working with young normal children.

We have attempted to present a program of activities in such a way that even an untrained person may begin activities that will aid the retarded child in growing and learning.

Believing that all children are entitled to an opportunity for maximum development of their potential, in a way that will bring satisfaction to themselves and help them to find an acceptable place in the communities in which they live, we are offering this book containing specific projects, based on sound psychological principles, which have helped many retarded children to develop socially, physically, mentally, and emotionally—and at the same time have fun!

BERNICE WELLS CARLSON
DAVID R. GINGLEND

ACKNOWLEDGMENTS

WE WOULD LIKE TO THANK the many parents of retarded children and professional people who have advised us, encouraged us, and inspired us to write this book, especially: Dr. Elizabeth Boggs, president, National Association for Retarded Children; Mr. Martin Papish, past president, NARC; Dr. Anna Starr, former head of Rutgers College Psychological Clinic and first professional advisor of Raritan Valley Unit, NJARC; Dr. Helen Donovan, assistant director, speech department, Bureau of Children with Retarded Mental Development, New York City; Miss Winifred Stiles, special music teacher, Plainfield, N.J., public schools; Mrs. Marion Meeks, physical education teacher, Plainfield, N.J., public schools; Mr. Harry Dubin, principal, Central School, and supervisor of special education, East Brunswick, N.J.; Miss Marian Shields, Mr. and Mrs. Christopher Maasch, Mr. and Mrs. Herbert Feist, and Dr. Carl W. Carlson.

CONTENTS

I. Need to Play

MOST RETARDED CHILDREN LIKE TO PLAY; AND WHEN THEY PLAY, they not only have fun, but usually develop physically, mentally, and socially—frequently beyond the realm of general expectation.

However, because they do not play spontaneously, because they have to be taught to play, this avenue of happiness is often closed to them. Far too many retarded children have spent hours just sitting, doing nothing, because no one has taught them how to play.

This is a great pity because retarded children can grow and learn through play in every area of development, just as normal children do—although the retarded child will be limited in his achievement. He may have handicaps of poor physical co-ordination and poor articulation in addition to, or as part of, his mental retardation, which may make it necessary to teach him in a slightly different way. He may have been rebuffed by society so that he has drawn within himself and is not using all the ability he has. Some people cannot realize that a big boy of twelve with a mental age of three may enjoy the same songs that a normal three-year old enjoys—if enjoying has not been discouraged by those whom he admires, his family, teacher, playmates, or other acquaintances.

13

Admittedly, it is hard to understand the retarded child because he is different. It is hard to help him. But understand him we must, and help him we can!

This book is written to help children with low mental age who, nevertheless, are capable of understanding a minimum of what is being said to them, capable of some degree of communication—by gestures if not by articulate speech—and who have some degree of muscular co-ordination which enables them to grasp, gesture, and move about.

However, this is not merely a "minimum" book. It is a book for growth. The first activities in each section are very simple ones which a child with extremely limited ability can perform. Other activities are then presented in the order of increasing difficulty. A parent or teacher must understand the child with whom he is working, find a project at his level, and help him to progress. This is difficult because a child's mental age may not agree with his social age or his physical age. A parent or teacher is advised to first choose an activity that he is sure a child can do and enjoy, and work from there on.

In general, we might say that this book may be used when working with children of a mental age of six years and under. However, children with mental ages of more than six may also enjoy a number of activities. They will sing songs better, play games better, and make more interesting handicraft than their more limited play-mates. This crossing of age levels in activities is not unique with retarded children. College boys, as well as nursery-school children, may enjoy singing "This Old Man" or "The Hokey Pokey." Girl Scouts make neater and more clever hospital tray favors than Brownies, even when both are using the same basic instructions.

The authors have seen a large variety of retarded children enjoying the activities described here—children at home with their families, in private-day classes, public-school classes, day camp, and in institutions. They have seen how these play ideas, when purposely used, have helped retarded children develop into happier children with more acceptable behavior and less dependence on others for care.

As the authors present each type of activity, they would like to show how it can help a child to grow and learn and how it helps to fulfill his basic needs. Therefore, we must first consider the basic needs of the mentally young retarded child.

BASIC NEEDS OF THE RETARDED CHILD

The needs of a retarded child are basically the same as those of his normal brother. He needs food, clothing, and shelter; and in the past has generally received them—and, all too often, little else. Like his normal brother, he needs spiritual, mental, and physical stimuli which will help him reach his full potential and help him to find an acceptable, and sometimes contributing, place in the society in which he lives.

LOVE. A retarded child needs to be loved, just as any child needs affection whether he is normal or handicapped, learning at home or in a classroom, living with his family or in an institution. He needs someone to talk to him, simply and patiently; someone to listen to him, even though his speech is most difficult to understand; someone to put an arm around his shoulder when he is disappointed. Most of all he needs a smile. When you play with him, smile! A smile signifies affection. It also helps to satisfy another great need—acceptance.

ACCEPTANCE. Everyone needs to feel that he is accepted. A retarded child needs to be accepted as he is, with all his limitations. Being part of a group, a family group or a class group, and doing things with other people can give this feeling of acceptance. The doing something may be as simple as helping mother to smooth out the wrinkles on a bed spread. In time, it may be playing a circle game or taking a trip.

Because of his limitations, a retarded child seldom joins a group spontaneously. He is like an infant who plays alone and has to learn to enjoy people around him. A retarded child must work into a group situation gradually—first the family, then a play group and, perhaps eventually, school and society at large. He will benefit greatly if he can also develop a feeling of religion, a sense that he is loved and accepted by God and that he has a place in the universe.

A retarded child must know exactly what he is expected to do. He deserves, and enjoys, praise when he does things "right." Receiving praise for doing something "right" is a sign of acceptance. It also satisfies another need—achievement.

ACHIEVEMENT. When we speak of the achievement of the retarded child, we have to accept a special philosophy of advancement. We cannot compare him with other children. We must accept each individual as he is and then look for each small sign of growth, rejoicing in it.

When a child who day after day has sat alone, showing no sign of emotion, at last faintly smiles as he accepts a proffered apple from his mother, he is achieving. If he eventually joins a circle of children playing a game, his achievement may be greater for him than a grade of one hundred on a test paper would be for his normal brother. If a child who has run ceaselessly and aimlessly around a room day after day, at last sits still in the family living room and listens to a record of music, he is achieving and his achievement should be recognized and praised.

To DEVELOP. Many retarded children have physical impediments. Their co-ordination is often very poor. Through games and handicraft, they may develop their muscles, large and small, and improve their co-ordination.

Retarded children develop mentally, but at a very slow rate. Mental achievement must be measured by each child's personal yardstick. Learning to listen, matching colors or objects, counting one-two-three are all mental achievements which may not come naturally but which can often be taught through play.

DO FOR OTHERS. A child needs to do for others. This is part of acceptance and part of achievement. He needs to help to set the table, to put the milk bottle on the porch, to scour a blackened pan until it shines. He needs to feel needed. As time goes

by, he may be able to make something that someone else can enjoy —perhaps a decoration for the family Christmas tree.

To CREATE. All people desire to create. Retarded children are not creative in the general sense of the word, although many of them have definite aptitudes for drawing, singing, or playing a musical instrument. As a rule, they do not originate ideas and execute them.

Yet, they find fun in "Doing something myself." This does not mean "all by myself." A parent or teacher must decide just how much she should do in advance and just when she should give assistance so that the child will have a satisfactory finished product and yet feel that the object is his because he worked hard on it. The adult may know that she drew a Christmas stocking, cut it out, and hemmed the edges. The child pasted pretty stars, all different colors, here and there on the stocking. The child made the stocking look pretty. He made it himself. He created it.

DISCIPLINE. A child needs discipline. There is an old saying "Too much freedom drives us wild!" Most certainly a retarded child finds too much freedom frustrating. He wants to know where he stands and what he can and cannot do and still be accepted in a class or by his family. He will have more fun in life when he has learned to follow rules. Games, handicraft, in fact all activities, have rules.

To BE A DEMOLITION ENGINEER. Someone once asked a very bright little boy what he wanted to be when he grew up and he quickly answered, "Demolition engineer." All children, including retarded children, want to be demolition engineers, although few can phrase their desires so accurately. Of course, a child must learn what to break and what not to break. A parent or teacher will have to find things which a retarded child can demolish. Quite obviously there are the breakdown toys which can be made or bought. There are plasticine clay objects which can be smashed into a ball after they have been admired. Cardboard boxes, after they are no longer needed for play, may be slashed down one side and a child may stamp on them to flatten them. Flat empty tin cans take up less space in a trash can than round ones. Remove both ends of tin cans. Ask the child to stand on them to flatten them. Or let him pound them with a mallet—out of doors. A retarded child need not be any more de-

17

structive than any other child. He can be taught to break only those things which he is asked to break.

To HAVE IDENTITY. A retarded child needs to be known as a person, a whole person, capable of enjoying life and giving enjoyment to others. Play with him. Help him develop. Help him to have fun.

GOALS FOR PLAY

Play is the work of childhood. It is as important to a child as a job is to a father and homemaking is to a mother. Almost everything that a child does is play, whether it is chanting "Patty Cake" or holding a dustpan while mother sweeps; and it is through this medium that a child becomes aware of himself as an individual person and aware of his relationship to the world around him.

Just as a father should have goals for his work and a normal child should have goals to meet in his academic program, so we who are teaching young retarded children, whether at home or at school, should set up goals for an activities program.

We know that retarded children do not learn naturally, as normal children do, by imitation and observation. They have to be taught to perform each task. They need understanding and sometimes help in order to get along with other people. They develop very, very slowly, advancing from one level to another gradually—from simple movements to organized play, from scribbled lines to handicraft projects. They may not develop evenly; a child may make big advances physically and poor social adjustments, or make noticeable advances mentally while becoming more, instead of less, immobile.

Therefore, in working with these children we must have a long-range and over-all point of view. We must start when a child is very young to do things that are worth doing and consistently follow those things which can be expanded. We must present each type of learning or skill in as many different ways and situations as possible and help a child to make as many meaningful contacts and to build up as many concepts as he can. Retarded children do exhibit a transfer of learning in a limited way if variations are introduced in a gradual fashion.

We must check frequently to see if a child is growing in all the ways that he can grow. It seems logical, therefore, to judge an activity program for a child in terms of his growth.

To do this, we may select areas in which a child should grow, check to see if each day's program includes activities which will aid the child's total development, and frequently look back to determine if a child is growing in each area.

We can frequently ask ourselves, "Why am I teaching this game?" "Why are we doing this handicraft?" "What are we gaining during this period of informal play?" As time goes on, we can change our activities program, just as we change the academic program to fit the needs of a normal child, in our effort to help him reach his full mental and physical potential and become a well-adjusted and useful person in the society in which he lives.

There seem to be five areas in which a young retarded child should continually be showing some signs of growth. We have attempted to briefly describe each of these areas and to pose questions which parents or teachers may ask to determine progress.

1. The Area of Mental Health This is the most important area. Without mental health, there is nothing. A lot may be said for the proverb "Happiness first; all else follows," especially if we consider the full meaning of happiness.

A child, whether at home or at school, should be in an atmosphere of acceptance where he can feel that he belongs and where he is with those who accept him as he is with all his abilities as well as his disabilities. Home or classroom should be a happy place where there is fun as well as work. Here a child should be presented with opportunities for achievement and a knowledge of success on his own level. Home or school should be a place where he can develop self-confidence, a feeling of belonging, and a feeling of security. It should provide opportunities to relieve tensions and overcome fears.

To judge growth in mental health we may ask:

Is he a happier child?

Is he easier to manage?

Does he exhibit more self-control?

Does he accept direction and authority more easily?

If he goes to school, does he like it?

19

2. *The Area of Social Development* This huge area, frequently mistaken for the entire program, has two aspects: adjustment of the child to the group and its leader, and the development of his ability to care for himself. In the former there should be development in the ability to share, work, and play with other individuals and with a group; an increased willingness to follow directions and to accept discipline; a growing eagerness to join in familiar group activities and to learn new activities. The group may be a small family or a class. The leader may be a parent or a teacher.

Social development also includes progress in self-help—dressing, feeding, and so on—, improved health and safety habits, increased interest span, increased ability to cope with stimulation, development of new interests and of willingness to play constructively alone and to think of pleasant things to do when no special activity has been planned for a designated time.

In judging development in this social area we may ask:

Does he work and play better with others? By himself?

Does he co-operate better?

Is he less easily distracted?

Is he happier in a group?

Is he more friendly when he meets someone new?

Can he do more things for himself?

Have his eating habits improved?

3. *The Area of Physical Development* Parents and teachers of retarded children have too often neglected this area, largely because of the safety factors involved. Most retarded children are clumsy; they do fall frequently; their muscles are not developed and their motor co-ordination is poor. Certainly sitting hour after hour, day after day, is harmful because unused weak muscles become weaker and motor co-ordination never develops by itself.

These retarded children need numerous daily activities that involve movement and the use of large and small muscles. There should be in each day's program many opportunities for a great variety of manipulations: walking, running, jumping, grasping, carrying, pulling, bending, stretching, rolling, lifting, dancing, and so on. Both free play and organized play should include opportunities to improve motor and muscular co-ordination, with the parents or teacher forever on the lookout for signs of overstimulation or approaching exhaustion.

Typical questions we might ask are:

Does he walk better?

Can he use his hands more effectively?

Has his co-ordination improved?

Can he use any play equipment that he couldn't use before?

Does he sleep more soundly?

4. The Area of Language Development This area is as important to a child without speech as it is to one with speech because language development includes more than making articulate sounds and because the fact that a child does not speak at the age when other children talk does not indicate that he cannot be taught to speak.

Language development includes listening and understanding as well as talking. A retarded child needs to learn to associate sounds with names of articles, with actions, with directions. Language development includes the ability to grasp the correlation between words and concepts: big and little, top and bottom, in and out, you and me, love and happiness.

A child who does not talk may need help in such simple acts as blowing a pinwheel, small boats in a pan of water, or the seeds from a full-blown dandelion. Blowing may be a prelude to speaking—as well as play. He may need help in tongue placement and lip movement in order to make certain sounds. Although speech therapy should be done by an expert in the field, a teacher or parent may

21

include many activities in a program which will aid in this area of language development.

Any advancement made in the ability to understand, to form sounds and associate them with sights, emotion, or action, or to communicate with verbal utterance may be accepted as growth in the area of language development.

Some questions we might ask are:

Does he seem to understand more of what you say?

Can he make his wants known more efficiently?

Does he verbalize more?

Does he speak more clearly?

Has his vocabulary increased?

5. *The Area of Intellectual Development* The area of mental development may center around a child's becoming more observant of things in his environment: his ability to notice things and remember, and his ability to hear things and remember. The first ability might be described as the development of visual discrimination and memory and include ability to work puzzles, to pick out things that are alike, to pick out something that is different than other things in a group, to match, to sort, to find what is missing from a familiar pattern, to reproduce patterns—numerous activities which involve observation and recall.

The second ability might be termed the development of auditory discrimination and memory. This would include the ability to follow spoken directions, identify rhythms and tunes, identify animal sounds, to finish a verse or story that has been told before.

Growth in this area is easier to judge than in some of the other areas because questions asked will center around the specific skills being taught.

As we work and play with our retarded children, let's stop often and determine whether we are using this medium to its best advantage to stimulate the child's total development.

APPROACHING THE PROGRAM

COMMUNICATION. Some people say that play "reaches" retarded children. This is because it affords a means of fulfilling many of their basic needs and also because it affords a means of communication. It is often very difficult to reach some of these children, and establishing a form of communication is as important to the parent or teacher as it is to the child. The slightest form of contact should be considered the beginning of a social relationship on which a more advanced social adjustment can grow.

Think back to the time when this retarded child you know was an infant. He didn't notice lights and sounds as other babies do. He didn't react to your voice or touch to any noticeable degree. Yet, you continued to give him brightly colored dangling toys and soft teddy bears and woolly blankets hoping to appeal to his sense of sight or touch. You talked to him, sang to him hoping to appeal to his sense of hearing. Then one day, as you played peek-a-boo with him, he evidenced pleasure. You had established a relationship, so you continued playing this peek-a-boo game. At last, he too gestured; and one day he played peek-a-boo!

This relationship which you had established was just as truly a social relationship as if he had asked you to play a game. An established social relationship gives a child the feeling of belonging, of being accepted, of having fun, of achieving. It helps him become aware of himself as a person and aware of his relationship to other people. This social relationship also gives him a feeling of security because now he has a "cushion" activity, something he can do and on which he can fall back and feel secure.

CUSHION ACTIVITIES. Discovering "cushion" activities and falling back upon them is an important factor in teaching retarded children. We must first discover what a child can do, and let him do it often. However, continued repetition of old activities will not lead to growth and, moreover, retarded children do become bored, as other children do. They need to be introduced to new activities; although when they are presented with a new play idea, they may become frustrated. A parent or teacher need not become discouraged. A child can try the new idea, and then fall back upon a "cushion" activity.

However, it is well to stop and appraise the new activity. Was it frustrating because it was too big a jump from a familiar activity? Was it within the scope of his physical and mental abilities? Did he understand what you wanted him to do? If the activity seems to fit

23

his abilities and is one which will help him grow, repeat it at a later date. It may eventually click; and if it does, it will be a big moment for the child! Enjoy his happiness and praise him.

Self-feeding, self-dressing, setting a table, as well as games and handicraft all fall into this category of new activities at one time or another in a child's development. Because a child cannot perform a task that other children his age have mastered does not mean that he can never do it. Thousands of adults in our institutions for mentally retarded persons are being fed by attendants each day. We'll never know how many might now be feeding themselves if they had been patiently encouraged to do so when young.

REPETITION AND ROUTINE. The world at large presents a very confusing picture to the retarded child. Home and school should not add to the confusion. Repetition and routine are two tools that help a child feel secure and at the same time venture forth.

We must never present too many ideas too quickly. We must present a new activity based on a known activity and give the child ample time to feel comfortable and familiar before we change a routine or introduce another new project. Many children entering a class have been conditioned to failure. They are timid, or overly aggressive, and have emotional problems which interfere with learning. They seem to sense that they are never doing quite enough and that some more difficult task is always waiting for them. Therefore, they refuse to do anything at all.

There is no magic clue about "what to do in a case like this" or "what to do now." Teaching of retarded children must forever remain creative with the parent or teacher sensing how to "reach" a child, where to start to teach him, when to repeat what he knows, and when to advance.

QUIET AND ACTIVE PLAY. Retarded children need active games to develop their muscles and also to "let off steam." Yet, many of them easily become overly stimulated and quickly discouraged. It is very important to set up a program of alternating active and sometimes noisy, activities with quiet and inactive play. Bodies and spirits respond well to this rhythmic pattern. Many discipline problems are avoided.

Many situations that might be overly stimulating at one time are well accepted at another. For example, can a retarded child have a party? That depends on the party as well as on the child. An elaborate birthday party with lots of strange children coming in, lots of noisy games, many gifts, and very fancy food would most certainly be too stimulating for a retarded child. (It can be too much for a young normal child.)

A special cooky, served with juice, can be a party. Some simple favors or decorations suited to the occasion, playing familiar simple games, singing well-known songs add to the fun. The party may be held at home, including only the family and perhaps a friend or two whom the child knows well, or at school.

As birthday celebrations become a part of the routine of living, they may become slightly more elaborate. Retarded children look forward to them as joyous occasions—as do all children. The same is true of other special things which a family or class may do. They should do something simple first, and progress from there. For example, a family or class might first take a walk to a near-by park. Much later, they might take longer and more stimulating trips, such as visiting a zoo or rodeo.

THE GROUP. As we have pointed out, the retarded child needs to be with others; for in a group, he gets the feeling of belonging, may develop acceptable social habits and attitudes, and also has fun. A child left alone and inactive may become withdrawn and fails to identify himself with his environment—which leads to mental illness.

A trainable mentally retarded child needs the association of other children who are closely allied to the same level of learning as himself. He also needs to associate with those who are above and below his level. Parents need to make him feel that he is an integral part of the family. They should also do everything possible to enroll him in a playgroup of children like himself—even if they have to organize and direct one. If the community in which he lives has any kind of special classes, either private or public, the child should be enrolled as soon as possible.

The world of the retarded child will always be a select and protected world—yet, it will be a world with different kinds of people in it. He will do well to learn how to get along with many kinds of people.

PLAYING ALONE. A trainable retarded child also needs to learn to enjoy working and playing alone. He can learn to play with cars, dolls, or other toys alone, and advance to a stage of make-believe. He can enjoy TV alone; for, despite the controversy about television, it has its good effects. Children learn to distinguish "goodies" and "badies," "cowboys and Indians." They imitate dancing, singing, and even acting. A child may listen to records alone.

CONTROL. We can point to at least two kinds of control—self-control and the willingness and ability to take orders from a leader— a parent or teacher. Both kinds of control improve as frustrations decrease.

A retarded child must know exactly where he stands. He should know exactly what is expected of him. He should know what behavior is acceptable and what behavior is not acceptable. There should be no exceptions. For example: banana peels go into some kind of container, never on the floor and never on the ground! This is true in our own kitchen or in the park.

If a child is capable of self-help, he should be allowed to wait on himself, glowing in the sense of achievement as he puts his thumb into the thumb of a mitten or ties his own shoe. Achievement is more important than time to a retarded child. Rushing is frustrating.

Once he has learned to play a game or set a table, he should be allowed to keep the same routine. One child always puts her shoes in a box when she takes them off in her room. They came from the store in a box.

Retarded children need opportunities to practice self-control, to feel that they are acting independently, while some adult is on hand and aware of the situation but not intervening—unless it is necessary. If a child reaches a point where he can make a decision, no matter how small, like putting fruit in a certain dish—and it is a socially acceptable decision, he should be allowed to carry out his plan.

Control of an individual or a group of children becomes possible when each child knows what is expected of him, can judge for himself when he is doing what is expected of him, and when activities chosen for him fulfill his basic needs.

SENSE OF PURPOSE. A person who is working with a retarded child must feel that what he is doing is important. He must feel that the project in hand is part of a long-time program and that its ramifications are more important than the skill learned or the project made in one day. For example, making an Easter basket is more important than just having an Easter basket at the end of a day. A child must also feel that what he is doing is important so that his actions may become increasingly purposeful.

27

II. Informal and Imaginative Play

ALMOST ANY KIND OF EXPERIENCE MAY BE ACTED OUT AND SO BECOME the subject for informal and imaginative play. If the family has visited Aunt Kate at her home, or the grocery store, or a farm, the scene may be re-enacted at home or in school. Retarded children like to play house and imitate cowboys or clowns whom they have seen on TV, just as normal children do. The difference is that retarded children do not instinctively imitate the people whom they have seen. They have to be taught how to use their imaginations and they need constant encouragement to do so. Therefore, this type of play should begin in the home with mother and child pretending that they are two mothers feeding or dressing the doll-child or father and son pretending they are driving a car, and so on. This pretending together helps to build a cozy family feeling which gives a child security. It helps him to develop his speech, express his emotions, and to move about.

This type of play should not stop with the home. It may be extended to an informal play group and to the classroom. In fact, informal and imaginative play should be included in any kind of play program for retarded children as it may do more than any other kind of play to help a young retarded child develop socially, mentally, emotionally, and physically.

Developing imaginative free play requires intuitive teaching and a certain atmosphere in which to grow and flourish. In a home, a parent cannot wait for a child to say, "Let's play house." She cannot regularly sandwich the play in between, say dishes and bed making. She must look for the little opportunities which constantly present themselves for imaginative play and take advantage of them.

"Now, you be the Mommy," she may say at bedtime. "Tuck the dolly in her bed. Cover her up. Kiss her goodnight." This is only a few seconds of play, but it's relaxed and it's fun and it may lead to other play moments of longer duration.

In a group, children seemingly play as they wish; yet control is always present. A parent or teacher is always there to give suggestions to enrich the play, or to divert or bring to a close play that is getting too active, exhausting, or over-stimulating to the point of disorganization. A wise parent or teacher can sense when to stay in the background, when to suggest, and when to participate. This is never a free time for the leader; he needs to be alert and observant of what is going on—yet, appear not to be.

Informal and imaginative play gives repeated opportunities for development of speech of all kinds, especially speech related to objects and action. First of all, a child develops an "inner speech"; he learns to understand more than he can say. Through play, he learns the meaning of place words, such as "here," "there," "in," "out," "on top of," "under." He may learn to interpret sense words such as "warm," "cold," "soft," "loud," "sharp." Simple conversation, used in play, usually includes giving and following directions, expressing feeling and emotions, and sometimes polite chit-chat.

Another of the goals in this kind of play is the development of self-control. In order to develop this self-control, a child must be given repeated opportunities to act as he thinks best in a relaxed, yet supervised, situation where there is a minimum of rules—no step by step direction. The opportunity to decide what to do next, to be able to accept or reject a suggestion, is important to growth; because if a

29

child is forced to constantly follow rigid regulations, if his every movement is controlled, he will eventually be able to function only in rigidly controlled situations. He will never be able to find his place in an average community where citizens follow directions, obey rules, and at the same time have repeated opportunities to amuse themselves in an acceptable manner.

This type of play strengthens a child's understanding of different social situations. His behavior in playing cowboys and rustlers will be very different than his behavior at an imaginary birthday party or a trip to a store. His play may also reveal to a parent or teacher his lack of understanding of basic social behavior.

Someone has said, in speaking about problems of normal adolescence, that adolescents need to be treated like adults long before they have become such. This principle applies to retarded children. In many ways they, too, must be treated as though they have reached a stage of development which has not yet been attained.

Informal play fills emotional as well as social needs. A retarded child is often tense, fearful of the future, worried about what you expect of him. Informal play helps him to relax, to work off tension, act out his problems. If he has a real problem about which he cannot talk, he may demonstrate his problem in his play; and, if the matter is not serious, a parent or teacher may be able to correct the situation. A child who is emotionally withdrawn may begin to express himself through informal play.

Informal play meets physical as well as emotional and social needs as it is the natural way to play. A child bends, stoops, or skips to the "store" as he feels the desire to do so. He is free to do what his body demands as long as he stays within the realm of acceptable behavior, respecting the rights of others, not damaging property—in general following the simple rules that have been set down and must be obeyed at home, school, or in any other social situation.

If a teacher wishes, she may guide this play around social subject themes such as "our home" or "our health"—real life situations. However, parent or teacher must always remember that informal play must be kept relaxed and free of rigid controls. It should always be labelled "play-time," particularly in an organized program.

PLAYING HOUSE, STORE, DOCTOR

Playing house, or store, or acting out any other of life's situations starts out very simply, usually in the home; but it has no limitations. A retarded child needs to be encouraged to "tuck the dolly in the little bed, all warm and feeling good," or to push the toy car "all the way along the road—*honk, honk*"; but once he has developed the idea of pretending, he may think of situations to act out.

At first he needs real props in his play; but later, like any other child, he can use some props and pretend he has others. A wagon may be a "Good Humor" car and the child will sell pretend ice cream, receiving pretend money. Chairs lined up in the kitchen may be a train, and the child will collect pretend tickets from whoever will ride. There can be a tea party with dolls as guests eating pretend food while mother and daughter engage in polite conversation with "please," "thank you," and "I had a good time."

Valuable as the parent-child make-believe play is, imaginative play is of greatest value when developed with a group of children because being in a group involves interaction and role playing. This group may be two or three retarded children playing at one home, or it may be a school group.

As you work with a group, don't expect that all the act-it-out activities will engross all the children all the time that the play is in progress. Some children will interact only briefly. Others will become completely absorbed. Often, there is a child who ignores the play all together.

Don't be concerned. There should be no compulsion to stay in an activity. A person doesn't have to play during a free-play activity period. He should be free to play as he wishes, perhaps with a toy by himself.

However, carefully watch the child who doesn't interact. He may be immature, not yet ready for social interaction, or playing together. He may be in the stage of "parallel play," best described as playing alone together. On the other hand, some aspect of free play is usually contagious, and the child who doesn't play may be withdrawn because he has some emotional problem.

As directing free play must be forever creative, there can be no

31

set rules for stimulating the activity. However, examples of how one teacher encourages free play may be helpful.

The House. A corner of the playroom referred to as "the house," is reserved for basic things used in this play—table, chairs, toy telephone, dishes, ironing board, clothesline, boxes holding dress-up material, and other household items. The number of things and their proportions is not important, except for table and chairs. Imagination is the element. Let no one tell you that retarded children do not have imagination in this kind of play! They reflect the world around them as they see it and reveal a surprising degree of understanding of attitudes and social situations.

New things, added to this corner from time to time, evoke a great deal of interest which is intense for a number of days and then wanes. When interest has waned, many of the things are put away; and after a period of time, gradually reintroduced and interest reactivated. Likewise, some new things are stored and brought out from time to time.

At the beginning of the day, the teacher says, "We have something new for the house—(and names it)." Everyone looks at it. Then it is placed in the house corner and work period begins.

Playtime is after lunch, before rest period. The children have learned to wait, looking forward to this time and not forgetting the new thing in the house. One morning, the "new thing" was two old pocketbooks. At lunch, one girl said, "I don't want any desert. I'm full!"

One of the smaller boys said, "I know what she wants. She wants to get at them pocketbooks." He was perfectly right!

Hospital. Another day, the new thing was a toy doctor's kit. For a week and a half after the doctor's kit was put in the house, the place became a hospital or a doctor's waiting room and office. Temperatures and pulses were taken. The rescue squad "sirened" around the room. A few strips of cloth were added for bandages. People were bandaged, got "needles," and so on. Once in a while, the teacher would ask the doctor or nurse, "What's wrong with him?"

"Measles," a child might say.

"Too bad," the teacher might say. "Have you given him a needle?" Or to the patient, "I hope you'll feel better soon."

If the activity is going full force, the teacher says and does nothing, except to observe and learn. Occasionally, he needs to broaden the activities. If he sees a child playing alone, he might say to another child, "Will you please see if his arm is broken. See if he would like to go to the hospital." If he doesn't want to go to the hospital, O.K. Maybe someone else would rather to go to the hospital than stay in the doctor's office.

Sometimes play is reactivated without preplanning. Some weeks after the hospital had been discontinued, the teacher was cutting collars from two old clean shirts to make smocks for painting. A child wanted to know what he was going to do with the collars. He buttoned one collar and placed it on a girl's head saying "There, Mary, is your nurse's cap."

The collars, after everyone had seen them, were placed in a box of dress-up materials. At playtime, the hospital play was reactivated with all of the original enthusiasm, but much more know-how. The teacher brought out what was left of the doctor's kit. Children asked for bandages. During the days of play that followed, the teacher made practically no suggestions.

Jail to Store. One day in playtime, the children were building an enclosure with big blocks. Asked what it was going to be, the boys said, "A jail."

The group had been playing jail for a few days, so the teacher remarked, "Oh, it looked like it was going to be a store," and walked away.

One of the children said, "Let's play store." (If the child hadn't made this comment, the project would have continued as a jail.)

However, store it was. The teacher brought out the toy cash register and the carton of cans which had been used in a store project earlier in the year. The cans had been opened wrong side up so that they looked like full cans when the label was right side up. They were placed near the block construction. Business flourished. Next day, the teacher brought out some mesh bags that had held oranges, bags he had been saving for a weaving project. The bags became shopping bags. Paper ones would have done. The house corner was reactivated. Dinners were cooked and served. People went to the store. Others placed orders by telephone and deliveries were made (at the suggestion of the teacher) .

Some other life situations which this group and other groups have acted out are: going to church, weddings, birthday parties, school, restaurant, picnic; being repair men, delivery men, salesmen, barbers, dentists, eye doctors, cops and robbers, cowboys and Indians; having a shoeshine; being in the Easter parade; visiting relatives, neighbors, and other friends; taking part in a talent or TV show.

Water Play. Many of the playhouse situations can involve playing with water which has value for learning and seems to relieve tension. Give a rubber doll a bath, talking about washing hands, ears, and so on. Wash doll clothes. Wash doll dishes. Pour water from a pitcher into a glass. Pour unused water into a sink or container when playtime is over.

TOY-TELEPHONE PLAY

Learning to use a toy telephone may be introduced either as informal play or as table work depending on how concentrated you want the activity to be. Use two toy telephones—one for the child and one for the parent or teacher. The adult rings a bell. The child is expected to lift his receiver and say, "Hello." The conversation then depends on the child's ability to talk and to follow directions.

The teacher usually says, "Hello. This is Mr. Ginglend. Who am I talking to?" The child gives his name and the teacher continues. "How are you?"

The answer is often, "Fine."

The teacher asks, "What were you doing when I called?" This may lead to a conversation about TV or free play. Then he may ask, "What is your mother doing?" Often the teacher asks, "Will you ask her something for me? Please ask her to come to the P.T.A. meeting." Or, "Please tell her that there will be no school tomorrow. It is a holiday." Or, "Please ask her to come and see me." Children enjoy the conversation. They repeat it in their free play and start free play centered around the conversation.

When the child has developed visual discrimination, he can be taught to dial a number. Print a number on a piece of paper. Teach him to match the numbers on the phone, from left to right.

PAPER-CARTON PLAY

Once a retarded child has grasped the idea of imaginative play, he can enjoy the land of make-believe dear to all children. Paper cartons are wonderful props.

With very little suggestion from a parent or teacher, a paper carton large enough for a child to sit in with his legs curled up may become a boat, a car, a train—anything. There is exercise in getting in and out of the box, curling up and getting comfortable. There may be conversation, too, or at least sound effects, as the boat *toot-toots*, the car *honk-honks,* or the train *choo-choos.* There may be interacting as the car leaves one place, with the driver saying "good-bye," and arrives somewhere else without changing position.

A carton may be a wagon, or a delivery truck, filled with toys or pretend groceries. It may be pushed to its destination; or with a string attached, it may be pulled.

A large carton may be a cave, a jail, a fort, a castle. A child can play alone, with a parent, or with a group of children in his land of paper-carton make-believe.

When the play is over and the carton has served its purpose, dismantle it, with the help of the retarded child! All children have a desire, an inner urge to smash things. Either let the child jump on the carton to break it, or slash the edges and let him finish wrecking it.

Tunnel Remove the flaps and the bottom from a cardboard carton large enough to hold a child in a sitting position with his legs curled

35

up. Set it on one side on the floor.

Ask, "What does it look like? A tunnel? Who can go through the tunnel?" The children, who want to, crawl through the tunnel on all fours. Then ask, "What e l s e goes through a tunnel?"

"A car, *h o n k-honk!*"

"A train, *choo-choo!*"

"A little bird, *peep, peep!*"

"A little rabbit, late at night, when everyone is asleep, *hop-hop.*"

"A big bear. He went under the mountain, not over the mountain."

In every case, a child will crawl through the tunnel on all fours, but he may approach the opening flying like a bird, hopping like a rabbit, or lumbering along like a bear.

Play House Make a playhouse out of a large carton that held an electric refrigerator. Cut out a door and windows, and let the children complete the project. Paint it with latex paint or a mixture of poster paint and soap flakes (not detergent) in the proportion of one half cup of paint to one tablespoon of soap flakes. Or rule the sides of the carton into bricks using a yardstick and making marks with black crayons. Color with red or multi-colored crayons.

Decorate the inside of the house. Paste painted, or cut-out pictures on the walls. Near the windows, staple (or fasten in some other way), curtains made out of cheese cloth or old sheeting.

Make a window box from a shoe box. Paint it. Cut slashes in the bottom. Invert it and insert construction paper or cardboard flowers. Attach it to the house beneath the window.

FURNITURE. Furnish the house with carton furniture. Children don't worry about proportions. A stove may be half as high as a table for all they care. To make a stove, invert a carton and paint burners on the top. To make a sink, remove the flaps from two cartons. Paste the bottoms of the cartons together. Use inverted cartons for stool and table. Let the children suggest what furniture they need for the playhouse. See if they can make it from cartons.

CUPBOARDS AND SHELVES. Glue cartons together to make cupboards for a playhouse or shelves for a toy store. Turn others upside down for kitchen counters or store counters.

When you no longer need the shelves or cupboard, lay the boxes flat on the floor. Let children step from box to box. They have to lift their legs. Later wreck the boxes.

Telephone Booth One day, when a teacher was dismantling a playhouse, he cut one side of the large carton and began to fold it into a smaller section.

"What's that?" asked a boy, spotting the folded carton.

"A telephone booth, John," said the teacher—the thought having just occurred to him.

"It's a telephone booth, a telephone booth," said the boy as he walked away. For three days, the partially dismantled carton was a telephone booth as the children made all types of calls, got change, talked to the operator, and so forth.

This is just one example of how a teacher or parent can take a clue from a child, change plans, and start a new and constructive informal activity.

Carton Tower Get a number of cartons which fit into each other. Have a child or children turn them upside down and pile them up for a tower. This requires using big muscles. Let them knock the tower down. Then, either build it up again, or fit the boxes one inside the other for storage.

Children can paint the boxes, or decorate them like many-colored wastebasket (page 113), and later use them for storage. Or a child can destroy the boxes at the end of tower play.

Fish Pond Cut out a large number of paper fish. Color or paint them. Fasten a paper clip or bobby pin on each one. Put them in a large cardboard carton "fish pond." Tie a small magnet onto the end of a string. Tie the other end of the string to a stick for a fish pole. Have the children take turns fishing. How many red ones, how many blue ones, how many yellow ones did each person get?

Funny You Cut off one side of a carton almost as high as a child is tall. Near the center top, cut a hole large enough for a child's head to fit through. Draw a body of any type of figure below. Let the child paint or color it.

The child places the bottom of the cardboard on his shoes, holds onto the sides of the cardboard, and sticks his head part way through the hole. He has to walk in a slightly stooped position in order to keep the cardboard on his shoes. A race with two or more "Funny You's" is hilarious and appeals to the children's imagination.

Space Man Remove the flaps from a cardboard carton large enough to slip over a child's shoulders. In the center bottom, make a hole large enough for his head to fit through. Make holes in the sides for arms. Use the box as it is, paint or color it, or cover with aluminum foil for a space man.

A child has fun pretending that he is a space man. He also learns to walk under restricted conditions.

BEANBAG AND OLD INNER TUBE PLAY

Beanbags and old inflated inner tubes are two pieces of inexpensive equipment which may be used in many ways and are safe for indoor and outdoor play. Beanbags are easier to catch than balls, and they "stay put" without rolling when they land after being tossed.

Make big beanbags six to eight inches square when finished, out of sturdy cloth. Fill them loosely with beans and sew them closed securely. A beanbag should make a pleasing "thud" when it hits an object or drops on the floor. It should be flexible enough to allow a person to get a good grasp and hold on when he catches it.

A child can play with an old inflated inner tube in many ways. He can roll it like a hoop. It won't mar a table or injure a child if it bumps into one. He can lie flat on it and pretend he is floating in the water. Or he can slip it over his shoulders and "chug-chug-chug" around the room, pretending that he is a tugboat. Two children can have a tug of war, each pulling on one side of the inner tube.

Both beanbags and inner tubes may be used in organized games and relays (pages 196, 202, 213).

Beanbag on the Head Place a beanbag on a child's head. Ask him to walk without touching it. Walk fast. Walk in time to music. He has to stand up straight to keep the beanbag on his head without touching it.

When it is time to go to bed, see if he can walk up stairs with a beanbag on his head. You can make a game out of doing something he may not otherwise want to do.

Beanbag Toss Place an old inflated inner tube on the floor. Toss a beanbag into the center of it. It will make a pleasing "thud" if it hits the side of the tube. Let the child toss. Have him stand farther away and toss again. Can he still toss the beanbag inside the tube?

Place a large, shallow carton on the floor. Have a child stand a short distance away and toss a beanbag into the carton. Increase the distance. Then try tossing the beanbag into smaller containers: a wastebasket, smaller cartons. Place three cartons of different sizes side by side. See if he can toss a beanbag into each carton. Place three cartons in a row, one behind the other. See if he can throw a beanbag into each carton.

THROUGH THE INNER TUBE. Hold an old inflated inner tube in the air like a hoop. See if a child can throw a beanbag through it. Have him try it up close, then farther away.

Clown face Remove the flaps from a cardboard carton. Turn it upside down. Draw a clown's face with a big mouth on one side. Cut out the mouth. Have the child paint or color the picture. Suspend a small bell from the top of the carton so that it hangs directly opposite the mouth.

Throw a beanbag into the open mouth. Try to ring the bell. If there are several players, take turns.

CLOTHESPIN PLAY

Fitting clothespins onto the edge of something requires considerable eye-hand co-ordination. You can make play out of it if you pretend that the finished project looks like something. Start with two-prong clothespins, either wooden ones or the smaller bright-colored plastic ones. Later use the snap-on type which are much more difficult to manipulate.

Let the child get the feel of the snap-on type before he tries to put them on anything. Make them *click, click* near his ear. Ask him to make them *click, click* near yours. He has to use his small finger muscles each time he clicks one, and you may be surprised to discover how weak these muscles can be.

Encourage a child to hang up clothes during playhouse play. Run clothespin relays (page 216).

Clothespin Fence or Castle Use any kind of empty tin can with a smooth edge. A can which has a lid, such as a tea can or candy can, gives extra practice in taking off the lid and later putting it on.

Have the child put two-prong clothespins around the rim of the can. What does it look like? A fence? Put plastic animals inside.

A castle? Many children have seen them on TV and in story books. Cut out a paper doll. Punch a hole in the top of her head. Tie her onto one end of a long string. Drop the doll into the castle, holding onto the other end of the string. Ask, "Where are you, little Princess? Come out, little Princess." Pull her out.

When the child has finished playing with the clothespins, he should put them in the can; and if there is a lid, put it on.

Fort Take the cover off a shoe box, or another box about that size. Cut a door in one side at the bottom of the box, leaving one side of the door uncut to make a hinge.

Have the child put clothespins, either two prong or snap-on, all around the edge of the box. Does it look like a fort? Most children have seen them on Western TV shows. Take a plastic horse, or an extra clothespin, and make him gallop, gallop into the fort. Shut the door. Don't let badmen come in!

Clothespin Road Show a child how to make a long road out of snap-on clothespins by snapping one clothespin onto one of the open ends of another clothespin. Have him snap many clothespins together, and set the line on the floor or on a big table. When laid one way, they look like a very bumpy road. If laid another way, they become a smoother road.

Make your fingers walk, walk, walk over the road. Encourage the child to imitate you. Pretend that your fingers are a little dog that says, "Bow, wow" as he runs! Or a cat that says, "Meow, meow!!" Or a big old cow that moves slowly and says, "Moo, moo!" Or a little caterpillar that creeps, creeps, creeps, and doesn't say a thing. Let a child choose what animal he would like his fingers to be as they travel over the smooth road, or the bumpy road.

CLOTHESPIN TRACKS. Help the child to lay snapped-together clothespins in parallel rows to form a railroad track. Have him *huff* and *puff* and "choo-choo-choo" as his fingers move like a train over the tracks.

41

BREATH-CONTROL PLAY

Activities which involve blowing are important in helping the retarded child to establish and strengthen breath control which is an adjunct to speech. There are many ways to include this activity in both informal and organized play.

Informal activities that involve blowing are usually of interest for only a short period of time. Therefore, a child should be given many opportunities to blow. Start with very simple activities similar to those listed below. Later try choral readings that use sounds instead of words (pages 55, 56, 58). Act out stories that call for huffing and puffing, like "The Three Little Pigs," or make up stories in which the wind howls around the house and the child makes the noise of the wind. Play a game (page 204) and run relays (pages 214, 217) which require blowing.

Blow the seed from a dandelion.

Blow out birthday candles, real or imaginary.

When you put antiseptic on small scratches, encourage the child to blow on it. It relieves the sting and takes the child's mind off the fact that it does sting.

Blow whistles and other instruments for sound effects.

Tear the end of the paper jacket that covers a drinking straw. Blow the jacket into the air. Pick it up, of course.

Blow up balloons.

If you have a party, use the type of favor which is curled into a tube with a feather on the end. When the child blows, the paper unwinds, makes a noise, and returns to its curled position.

Blow up paper bags and make them pop.

Blow brightly colored pinwheels. See the color and design change!

Blow soap bubbles, the old-fashioned kind, with a clay or corn-cob pipe, or with a new plastic pipe with which you can blow one to four bubbles simultaneously. Make your own soap bubbles. Add two tablespoons of glycerine to a pint of soapy water to make bubbles have pretty colors. Or paint the inside of a clay pipe with water color to make pretty colored bubbles.

Blow Gun Make a blow gun out of a cardboard tube—a toilet-tissue tube or a larger wax-paper or paper-toweling tube. Crumple

tissue paper into a ball slightly less in diameter than the tube. Tie the wad with brightly colored thread, if you wish.

Load a wad into the gun. Have the child blow on one end of the tube and and see the paper wad fly out. Now, see how far away the wad can be blown. See how far into the air it can be blown. Try to blow the wad into a container. Step farther away from the container. Blow again. See if the child can blow the wad into a smaller container.

If the child likes the blow gun and wants to keep it, let him paint or color it.

Little Boats in a Dishpan Sea Make little paper boats like Soldier's Hat (page 119) only much smaller. Or make Bottle-Top Boats (page 151). Place a boat in a large pan of water, like a dish pan. Encourage a child to blow the boat around the "sea." Place two boats in the water next to each other. Blow. See if one boat gets across the pan before the other. If two people are playing, stand on opposite sides of the pan. Place a boat in front of each player. See who can blow his boat across the pan, and at the same time keep the other boat from landing on his side of the pan.

STORM AT SEA. Make a storm at sea. Take a large tube, about 1/2 inch in diameter, or a short length of hose about that size. Put one end in water. Blow up a storm. Make the water gurgle and bubble. Let the child blow up a "storm." See if he can sink a boat.

Do not blow up a storm with soda straws! It prompts children to blow into milk or soda to make bubbles—a very undesirable habit! When retarded children use larger tubes, they do not usually transfer the activity to blowing milk or soda.

Blow Them Over! Make several paper figures which a child can blow over. Cut a piece of fairly heavy paper—construction paper, typing paper, or wrapping paper— into a rectangle 3 inches wide and 6½ inches long. Fold under a 3-inch square for the base. Draw a figure of a cat, clown, rabbit, or anything else, on top part, leaving a wide base. C u t around the figure. Line the figures up on a desk or table. Have a child  stand in front of the figures with his hands behind his back. Ask him to blow. How many figures toppled over? Blow and blow again. Blow all the figures off the table. Set the figures up again. Take a big breath. How many figures can the child topple over with one breath?

Put the figures on a chair. A child has to stoop or bend in order to blow. See how many he can blow over now with one breath. Blow the figures with a blow gun (page 42). This requires pointing the gun and then blowing. If there are several players, have Blow Them Over Relay (page 214).

VIGOROUS PLAY

Retarded children need vigorous play—running, jumping, and play which includes the use of equipment such as swings, jungle gyms, slides, and so on—just as all children need this type of play in order to develop large muscles and to let off steam. They need supervision from start to finish.

At first a retarded child is afraid to try equipment, unsure of himself as he tries to maneuver his body into different positions or to hold onto something really tight. A patient parent or teacher can help him overcome this fear, staying with him as he plays, helping him, watching him as he ventures forth alone.

But once the child ventures forth on his own, the parent or teacher must be increasingly watchful. Frequently, when the child's fear is overcome, he is so delighted with his achievement that he throws safety to the wind. Safety factors must be carefully taught and rigidly insisted upon under the constant supervision of an adult. It takes lots of experience and many reminders before safety rules become habits.

Because vigorous activity is tiring, half an hour or less of this type of activity is enough—especially in its early stages.

Using Playground Equipment

SLIDE. Try a small slide first, not higher than an adult is tall. Have the child climb to the top with the adult standing on the ground close by, holding the child if necessary. When the child reaches the top, he sits down, with the adult holding him. The adult keeps his arms partially around the child as he goes down the slide.

SWING. The important thing when learning to swing is to have a swing low enough to allow the feet to touch the ground. It gives security. Retarded children are most comfortable in swings that have backs. If a swing does not have a back, and a child is fearful, hold him during his first experience with swinging. When the child is ready to sit in a swing alone, push him gently and urge him to "hold on tight," so that he doesn't fall out backwards. It takes a long time for a child to learn to swing using his body to gain momentum.

Swings which look like horses and are pushed with the feet are excellent for muscular development.

SEESAW. Children find it easy to seesaw. Watch carefully to make sure that one child doesn't get off allowing the other end to drop with a "thud."

JUNGLE GYM. Stay beside a child on a Jungle Gym. Encourage him to hold on tight as he climbs. Make sure that he doesn't suddenly let go and fall.

Digging Retarded children profit from digging, both in a sandbox and in the earth. A child can become completely absorbed in sandbox play for a long period of time. Give him an old sifter and a toy dump truck to fill and empty. Give him a certain number of cups or small pans. Count them—one, two, three. Have him bury them in the sand. Then find them again—one, two, three.

Wet the sand. Show him how to mound it up and dig a tunnel through the bottom of the mound. Make "pies" in containers. Unmold them.

If the locality permits, find a spot where he can dig with a small sturdy shovel in soft earth. Let him make mud pies after getting your permission to get dirty.

Hammering Every child loves to pound. It satisfies a physical need and relieves tension. There are many commercially made "knockout" toys with which he can play. He also needs a real hammer and a chance to just pound.

Try to get a section of a tree trunk and stand it on end. Let him pound nails into it, anywhere, and pull out the bent ones with a claw hammer. Or get a log and place it on its side, or a box made of soft wood placed bottom side up. Have the child hold the hammer near the head when he is learning. Start him with roofing nails and gradually decrease the size of the nail head and increase the length of the nail as he becomes more competent. When he has learned to pound, encourage him to do craft work (page 129-131).

SPLASHING AND SWIMMING

There is something very pleasant about water. It is quieting and stimulating at the same time. Taking off shoes and walking in the wet grass on a summer morning gives a sensory pleasure which somehow is soothing to the nerves. Wading, or dangling one's feet in a pool, lake, or other body of water gives the same sensation. Playing in water seems to benefit all types of children. The fearful child discovers that he can push it, and it gives way; and he gains confidence. The overly aggressive child discovers something which he can push and punch to his heart's content; and no one objects. Certain muscles can best be developed in water.

There must be water rules, and they must be strictly enforced. They are necessary for safety. They also give children a sense of security. A child will venture forward, if he is sure that he isn't going to be pushed from behind.

Don't force a child to go into the water or urge him too strongly. Let him sit at the edge of the pool, dangling his legs in the water or kicking up a "storm" until he is used to the situation and wants to join in the fun. If he will stand in the water, show him how to cup his hands, blow through them, and make the water bubble and "boil." Give him a life jacket or inner tube and show him how he can float.

There are many ways to encourage a child to get himself wet. Pretend that you hate to get wet. Children will splash you, and get themselves wet in the process. Play "Ring Around the Rosie." The children are sitting before they know it. Play "Red Rover" (page 196) in the shallow end of the pool. Many retarded children learn to swim once they have learned to like the water.

Don't overdo this vigorous water play. Many retarded children get exhausted quickly and chill easily. An hour of water-play has proved to be enough for any group of retarded children.

HELPFUL PLAY

Almost anything a child does around the house with someone is play for him; he especially enjoys activities involving vigorous action. He should have someone with him while he is working so that he can talk about what he is doing.

Window Pictures Cover a window with the type of window wax or powder that leaves a heavy film. Wrap a rag around a child's finger, or let him work with a bare finger. Encourage him to make lines up and down, zigzag or circles (see painting page 105). Or make a

47

picture. When the window is decorated, rub it hard. Get off all the wax. Make another picture on another window some other time.

Tin-Can Smashing Tin cans which are flattened after the ends have been removed take up very little room in a trash can. Elect your retarded child "Official Tin-Can Smasher." Remove the bottom as well as the top of the can. Set the can on the floor and have him stamp on it. Or ask him to take it outside and pound it with a wooden mallet.

Scouring Scouring a blackened pan uses many muscles, big and small. It's surprising and rewarding to see the black disappear as the pot gets shiny.

Waxing Retarded children can help wax almost everything that has to be waxed. Paste wax is best as retarded children have difficulty in applying the liquid type. Give a child a small damp cloth. He rubs it on the wax and then on the surface to be polished. As the wax is dull, he can easily spot places he has missed. Give him a soft cloth and encourage him to "rub, rub, rub" and make it "shine, shine, shine" until he can see himself in the surface.

To wax large surfaces, use a brick that is securely wrapped in carpeting so that it won't come out, and then wrapped with a soft cloth. The brick provides the weight and pressure which the little hands cannot. However, the child can and usually likes to push the brick back and forth across the surface.

Most fun of all is polishing an already waxed surface by skating on it. Wrap old towels around a child's feet. Then have him slide, slide, slide, or *choo-choo-choo*, all around the floor.

III. Follow the Leader and Choral Speaking

PLAY, LIKE ALL LEARNING, MUST DEVELOP GRADUALLY FROM A simple, unorganized form without apparent direction to a more organized form dependent upon direction and rules. A child must learn, step by step, to accept leadership and to follow directions.

The first leaders whom he knows are his parents, and perhaps his brothers and sisters. Many of the follow-the-leader and choral-speaking activities given here lend themselves to genuine family fun. Children are fascinated when adults enter enthusiastically into games. This type of activity provides an example to imitate, adds verve, and helps a child to accept directions. It also seems to help a child to feel that he is a part of the strange world of adults.

Learning at home to pay attention, listen, and translate what he hears into action are valuable assets for a child when he enters an organized play group or class in school. Activities of this kind are continued and expanded in a good school program.

The values of learning to follow acknowledged leadership are self-apparent. Many retarded children must be told what to do and how to do it all their lives. Learning to follow when told to follow, to speak when told to speak, and so on, will most certainly help them to live in any environment.

49

HANDIES (FINGER PLAYS)

Often a child will pay attention to a leader's hands before he will pay attention to what he is saying. Herein lies one of the great values of handies, or finger plays—acting out a little verse with hands as you speak. Handies also encourage a child to use small finger muscles that often remain comparatively inactive.

Before you start this type of play, remove from sight any toys or gadgets which might distract a child's attention. Sit or stand directly in front of the child. Speak to him clearly and in a well-modulated voice. Ask him to do as you do; and if you expect a response, to say what you say. At first he may not be able to say the words, but will enjoy the hand movements. Later he may be able to speak with you, imitating the movement of your lips as well as your hands.

You can use familiar verses, or you can use new ones. You can also use musical finger play (pages 163-66). You can play with one child, or with a group.

Two Little Blackbirds The leader chants the verse. Leader and children do the actions.

Two little blackbirds	(*Clench fists, thumbs sticking up.*)
Sitting on a hill.	
One named Jack.	(*Wiggle left thumb.*)
One named Jill.	(*Wiggle right thumb.*)
Fly away Jack.	(*Flap left arm with big movement and thumb wiggling. Put fist behind back.*)
Fly away Jill.	(*Flap right arm with big movement and thumb wiggling. Put fist behind back.*)
Come back Jack!	(*Bring left fist forward. Wiggle thumb.*)
Come back Jill!	(*Bring right fist forward. Wiggle thumb.*)

Here's the Church Leader and children say the verse and pantomime the action with indicated finger movements.

Here's the church.	(*Interlock fingers. Turn hands over to make a flat surface.*)
Here's the steeple.	(*Raise pointer fingers to form point.*)
Look inside;	(*Turn hands over to show interlocking fingers.*)

See all the people!

First they sing.   *(Open hands and hold palms toward you like an open book.)*

Then they pray.   *(Hold hands as if in prayer.)*

Then they slowly   *(Wiggle fingers like people walking away.)*

Walk away.

Creepy Bug [1] Put your left arm straight out. Your right fingers are a creepy bug. Move them up your arm as you say the verse.

Creepy bug goes up and up,   *(Move fingers rather fast up extended arm.)*

And up, and up, and up.

And all around your head.   *(Move fingers slowly around neck.)*

And down and down.   *(Move fingers rapidly down arm.)*

And down and down.   *(Drop arm suddenly.)*

Woops!   *(Shake off imaginary bug.)*

He's dead!   *(Step on it.)*

The Little Fish Doing two different things at the same time is difficult for retarded children. However, it's a skill that comes in very handy. Practice the motions in "The Little Fish" step by step. Then add the verse.

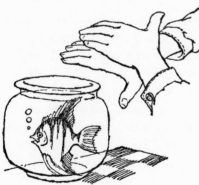

(Put your left hand out, palm down, fingers closed and thumb sticking out. Put your right hand on top of your left, palm also down and thumb sticking out. See the fish with fins at his sides. Wiggle your thumbs. Make the fish swim by moving hands up and down in unison. Now, make the fish swim and wiggle his fins at the same time.

[1] By Marian Meeks.

Open his mouth. Keep the palms together, but drop the left-hand fingers and raise the right-hand fingers.)

Little fish	(*Put palms together in above position.*)
Goes out to play.	
He wiggles his fins,	(*Wiggle thumbs.*)
Then swims away.	(*Move fingers up and down in unison.*)
He swims and swims	(*Move fingers up and down in unison and wiggle thumbs.*)
In the water bright.	
He opens his mouth	(*Keep palms together. Lower fingers of left hand. Raise fingers of right hand.*)
And takes a bite.	(*Close to starting position.*)
Mmmmmmm! Tastes good!	

DO WHAT I DO

There is an endless variety of games where players follow the leader, doing as he does under various conditions. These games may be played anywhere. At home, a parent is the leader. At school, the teacher is the leader. There may be one other player, or there may be several. The leader may be standing or sitting in front of a child or a group.

The leader may introduce any movement he wishes to develop muscles. For example: he may say, "Now, we'll fly like birds." He makes big flapping motions with his arms, but stands still. Everyone imitates him. Later players may form a line and fly like birds, following the leader across the lawn or around a room.

Participants may march, with or without music, changing actions at the command of the leader. The leader may call out, "Beat the drum!" All pantomime beating the drum. "Lead the band!" "Blow the horn!" Players may sometimes chant a verse as they follow the leader, thus combining speech and action.

Follow-the-leader games, like all other games, should be fun— not calisthenics. Stop the game before anyone gets tired.

Hold onto the Rope Retarded children need to learn to keep in line. They may have to stand in line to be served at a cafeteria, to board a bus, or to buy a ticket for a movie. They must learn to walk in line for air-raid and fire drills or when they take walks as a class. They will form lines to play certain games.

One way to teach children to walk in line is to have each one grasp a long rope with his left hand, then walk together. They may sing as they walk.

Tune: "Row, Row, Row Your Boat"

> Hold, hold, hold the rope.
> Do not let it fall!
> Merrily, merrily, merrily,
> Follow one and all!

Children can also hold onto the rope and pretend that they are a team of horses. Put the slowest children at the head of the line.

Snail, Snail Sometimes retarded children gain the concept of line when they walk around a definite object, such as a table, when playing a game. To be a snail, each child puts his hands up and over his shoulders and bends over as he walks. This position requires using big back muscles.

When children are in line, they walk very slowly, like snails, and say:

> Snail, snail, creep into your shell.
> Snail, snail, follow well.
> Wind, wind, keep in line;
> Follow the leader; keep in line.

Clap in Time Clapping in rhythm requires concentration and a certain amount of memory work. Practice it only for a short period of time, but use it frequently.

The leader always says, "We are going to clap like this," and demonstrates. Then the children clap with him in the same pattern he has illustrated.

Develop patterns of short rapid claps, and a big clap. Start with a clear: 1—2—3. When the children follow this well use a more complicated: 1-2-3; 1! A lone clap is always a big clap. Try 1-2-3; 1-2-3; 1-2-3; 1! Or 1-2-3; 1! 1-2-3; 1! 1-2-3; 1-2-3; 1-2-3; 1-2-3; 1! It may take some time before they can do the last.

Use clapping throughout the day. For example, when Peter has won a race, say, "We'll give Peter a big clap. Like this." Demonstrate. Then everyone claps while Peter enjoys being the center of attention—a wonderful reward for a race well run. A losing team may clap for a winning team after a game. Children may say, "Thank you," by giving a big clap for someone who did them a favor, like bringing cookies for a party surprise. At the end of a clap, the group is always in order and ready to receive your next instruction.

Freddie's Friend The leader tells a story about a child. The leader and the child or children in the group do what the child in the story does.

Freddie sat down. (*Sit down.*) He was all alone. He wanted a friend to play with him. He saw a bird in the sky. Freddie stood up. (*Stand up.*) He waved to the bird. (*Wave.*)

The bird didn't see Freddie. Freddie sat down. (*Sit down.*) He was still alone. He saw an airplane in the sky. Freddie stood up. (*Stand up.*) He waved to the airplane. (*Wave.*) The airplane didn't see Freddie. Freddie sat down. (*Sit down.*) He was still alone.

Freddie saw a puppy dog. Freddie stood up. (*Stand up.*) He waved to the puppy dog. (*Wave.*) The puppy dog saw Freddie. Freddie motioned, "Come here!" (*Beckon with full arm.*) The puppy dog ran to Freddie. Freddie sat down. (*Sit down.*) The puppy dog put his nose in Freddie's lap. Freddie petted the puppy dog (*Pet imaginary dog.*) Freddie wasn't alone. He had a friend.

CHORAL SPEAKING

Don't let the term "choral speaking" frighten you. It merely means making a noise or saying something in unison. And don't wait until a child can speak before you try using one of these activities. You can introduce choral speaking as soon as you believe that a child can pay attention and can comprehend most of what he hears.

Read a simple verse with only a phrase in the refrain. Speak clearly and in a rhythmic tone. Wait for the child to join you in the refrain. If he doesn't respond, say the refrain yourself, and continue. He'll join you when he feels at home in the situation. If you have a small group, some children will join you; others will copy them when they are ready.

Start with a verse that doesn't require a word in the refrain. In "Molly-O, the Fish Who Would Blow," the listeners merely blow. No one can be embarrassed if he comes in at slightly the wrong time, because he doesn't make a sound. Follow with verses that require howling, or making animal or other noises. Eventually use verses which require saying words.

Besides being fun, choral speaking aids in developing breath control (page 42) a very important factor in speech. It increases interest span, and helps to teach a child to listen and respond. Saying something in a group helps to give a child self-confidence. Notice how proud a child seems to be when he has learned how to respond. See how he will watch your mouth and try to imitate you.

Molly-O, the Fish Who Would Blow Practice blowing before you do this choral speaking. Blow gently. Blow hard. Follow the leader, blowing in rhythm with him. The leader reads the verse. Everyone blows when the leader comes to the words "blow" which are printed in italics. They blow gently. They blow hard, according to the directions and the sense of the verse.

There once was a fish, named Molly-O;
She wouldn't say yes, and she wouldn't say no;
But, oh, my goodness! How she would blow! *BLOW, BLOW, BLOW.*
(*hard*)

When she was glad she would *blow, blow, blow,* (*gently*)
But a fisherman's hook made her *BLOW, BLOW, BLOW.* (*hard*)
Little fish in the sea copied Molly-O.
She taught them all to *blow, blow, blow.* (*gently*)
When a fisherman's hook, dropped down below,
They puckered their mouths and went *BLOW, BLOW, BLOW.* (*hard*)
"When you see a hook, please let it go!
"Don't take a taste," she said, "just *BLOW, BLOW, BLOW!*" (*hard*)
Now Molly-O still swims in the sea
Because she can blow like you and me. *blow, blow, blow* (*gently*) and
  BLOW, BLOW, BLOW (*hard*)

The Witch on a Windy Night Practice making the sound of the
wind. Move your index finger in a big circle as you say, *"Shuuuuuuuuuuuu!"* The leader reads or says the verse and the children
join in making the sound of the wind. On second reading, they may
be able to join the leader in saying the last line of each verse. When
they come to the climax, they may want to clap their hands and
say, "Bang!"

An old witch sat at home all alone;
Cooking and cooking a big soup bone.
And the wind blew all around the house. *Shuuuuuuuuuuu!*

"Oh, who will share my soup," she crowed.
"If I drink it all, I'll surely explode!"
And the wind blew all around the house. *Shuuuuuuuuuuu!*

A big dog barked at her front door;
"Go away!" she said, "I chased you before!"
And the wind blew all around the house. *Shuuuuuuuuuuu!*

A bat flew up to the window pane.
"Go away, bat! Stay out in the rain."
And the wind blew all around the house. *Shuuuuuuuuuuu!*

"Oh, will you share your soup with me?"
The black cat purred, "With me? With me?"
And the wind blew all around the house. *Shuuuuuuuuuuu!*

"I've changed my mind! I hate to share!
"Let everyone starve for all I care!"
And the wind blew all around the house. *Shuuuuuuuuuuu!*

"I'll drink the soup myself," she sang.
What happened then? She exploded. Bang!
And the wind blew all around the house. *Shuuuuuuuuuuuu!*

They Lived in a Barn The leader reads the verse. Children join in making the noises or mouthing the words silently, as directed.

There was a little cat that said— (*Meow, Meow*).
There was a little dog that said— (*Bow, Wow*).
There was a little bird that said— (*Peep, Peep*).
And they lived in a barn that couldn't say a word. (*Shake head and silently mouth, "Couldn't say a word."*)

The cat saw the bird, and said— (*Meow, Meow*).
The dog heard the cat and said— (*Bow, Wow*).
The bird heard the dog and said— (*Peep, Peep*).
The barn heard it all, but couldn't say a word. (*Shake head and silently mouth, "Couldn't say a word."*)

The cat chased the bird and said— (*Meow, Meow*).
The dog chased the cat and said— (*Bow, Wow*).
The bird flew away and said— (*Peep, Peep*).
The barn saw it all and couldn't say a word. (*Shake head and silently mouth, "Couldn't say a word."*)

The cat was sad and said— (*Meow, Meow*).
The dog was glad and said— (*Bow, Wow*).
The bird was glad and said— (*Peep, Peep*).
The barn was glad, but couldn't say a word. (*Shake head and silently mouth, "Couldn't say a word."*)

The cat ran away and said— (*Meow, Meow*).
The dog went out to play and said— (*Bow, Wow*).
The bird found another home and said— (*Peep, Peep*).
The barn couldn't move, and couldn't say a word. (*Shake head and silently mouth, "Couldn't say a word."*)

Sometimes I play I'm a cat and say— (*Meow, Meow*).
Sometimes I play I'm a dog and say— (*Bow, Wow*).
Sometimes I play I'm a bird and say— (*Peep, Peep*).
Sometimes I play I'm a barn, and don't say a word. (*Shake head and silently mouth, "Don't say a word."*)

57

After children have learned to do this verse in choral speaking, let them act it out. Choose characters for the cat, dog, bird, and barn. They sit near the leader, without moving, and give the response. Later, let them go through the actions as well as the sounds. The cat chases the bird, but never catches it. This requires understanding and discipline! The barn doesn't move, and doesn't say a word.

Wally Wally, the Car Who Could Toot Before you read this story, explain that it is about Wally Wally, a car that could toot. However, he only tooted at the right time, and he only tooted twice, *toot, toot,* just two times. Give each child a horn and see if he can toot when you say, "toot." Toot two times, *toot, toot.* Toot softly, *toot, toot.* Toot loudly *TOOT, TOOT.*

The leader reads or tells the story. He pauses when the car says, *toot, toot.* The child or children blow the horns.

Wally Wally was a pretty blue car. He had a little horn that said (*toot, toot*). When he passed a friend and wanted to call, "Hi, there!" he said (*toot, toot, gently*). When he wanted to yell, "Watch out!" he loudly said (*TOOT TOOT!*).

Wally Wally was very polite. Whenever he passed another car, he would quietly say (*toot, toot*). One day, when Wally Wally was driving down town, a little boy ran into the street to get his ball. He didn't look to see if a car were coming. Wally Wally shouted (*TOOT, TOOT!*). The boy stopped and waited until Wally Wally had passed.

Another day, a little girl was riding her bike and forgot that she should stay near the curb. She started to go into the middle of the road. Wally Wally shouted (*TOOT, TOOT!*).

Oh, Wally was glad that whenever there was danger he could yell (*TOOT, TOOT!*). He was glad that when he met a friend he could politely say (*toot, toot*).

VARIATION. In this story and the one that follows, children may say "honk, honk" instead of blowing horns, *"toot, toot."*

Wally Wally in the Country Make up other stories about Wally Wally, the car who could toot. Include animal sounds as well as the horn. The story can go on as long as the child is paying attention. When interest wanes, cut it short.

One day Wally Wally went for a ride in the country. In a green field he saw a big brown cow who said *(Moo, Moo)*. Wally Wally answered, *(toot, toot)*. Then Wally Wally saw some pigs. They were so busy eating that they only said *(Oink, Oink)*. Wally Wally politely said *(toot, toot)*.

A little farther along Wally Wally passed some woolly woolly sheep. They looked up and said *(Baa, Baa)*. Wally Wally answered *(toot, toot)*. Soon Wally Wally passed a barn and a big red rooster who said *(Cock-a-doodle-do!)*. Wally Wally said *(toot, toot)*.

Suddenly Wally Wally felt very tired and stopped under an apple tree to rest. A pretty red bird flew down, sat on Wally Wally's engine, and said *(Peep, Peep)*. Wally Wally answered very quietly *(toot, toot)*. This scared the pretty red bird. She flew away.

Wally Wally took a nap. He couldn't snore like you and me. He said *(toot, toot)*. At last, Wally Wally woke up. He hoped he would see the red bird sitting on his engine. Instead he saw a snake that said *(Hiss, Hiss!)*. Wally said *(toot, toot)*. A snake can't hurt a car! The snake slithered away. Wally Wally laughed, and said *(toot, toot)*. "I'm going home. Good-bye animals and bird in the country, and little snake. Good-bye," he said *(toot, toot)*.

Before We Play The leader says a line very clearly. Children repeat it, making suggested motions.

A A	*(All have hands folded.)*
What shall we play?	
E E	
What will it be?	*(Open palms in questioning gesture.)*
I I	
Point to the sky.	*(Point to the sky.)*
O O	
The ground is below.	*(Point to the ground.)*
U U	
What shall we do?	*(Fold hands again.)*
E E	
What will it be?	*(Open palms again.)*

At the end of the verse, children choose an activity.

Advanced children may add a line, substituting it for the last line.

A E I O U
Let's do something new!

A A-What Shall I Say? Use a rhyming choral response in which the children do not know what the leader will say, because he changes it each time he does it. This requires marked attention as a listener cannot depend on rote. The leader says a line clearly. Children repeat it after him.

A A
We sing every day.
We swim in the bay.
We're happy and gay.

E E
Diddle dum dee!
Buzz like a bee.
Drink up your tea.

I I
Let's all say, "Hi!"
I like cherry pie.
Let's wave good-bye.

O O
The green light says, "Go!"
The red light says, "No!"
Wiggle your toe.

U U
Point to your shoe.
Say, "How do you do!"
The cow says, "Moo."

A A
Let's shout, "Hurrah!"
It's enough for today. (*Clap hands at end of verses.*)

A Bear Hunt The leader says each line in a rhythmical manner. Children and leader repeat each line together, making the necessary motion.

I want to go on a bear hunt. (*Children repeat each line.*)

All right!

Let's go! (*Slap thighs with hands.*)

Oh, look!

There's a brook.

Can't go round it. (*Make a "go round" motion with hand.*)

Can't go under it. (*Make a "go under" motion with hand.*)

Can't go over it.

(*Make "go over" motion with hand.*)

Gotta go through it.

All right!

Let's go. (*Make swimming motion.*)

Oh, look!

There's a bridge.

Can't go round it. (*Make "go round" motion with hand.*)

Can't go under it. (*Make "go under" motion with hand.*)

Gotta go over it.

All right!

Let's go! (*Thump chest with both hands as you go over bridge.*)

Oh, look!

There's a swamp.

Can't go round it. (*Make "go round" motion with hand.*)

Can't go under it. (*Make "go under" motion with hand.*)

Can't go over it. (*Make "go over" motion with hand.*)

Gotta go through it.

All right!

Let's go! (*Slide hands together.*)

Oh, look!

There's a tree.

Can't go over it. (*Make "go over" motion with hand.*)
Can't go under it. (*Make "go under" motion with hand.*)
Gotta go up it.
All right!
Let's go! (*Motion with both hands climbing up and down tree.*)
Oh, look!
There's a cave.
Let's go see
What's inside?
All right!
Let's go! (*Tramp softly; lower voices on next lines.*)
Let's go softly.
Let's go quietly.
Oh, look!
I see two big eyes.
I see two big paws.
I feel something like a fur coat.
It looks like a bear.
It feels like a bear.
IT IS A BEAR! (*Loudly*)
Let's go! (*Tramp fast with feet.*)
Up the tree. (*Make fast motion up the tree.*)
Down the tree. (*Make fast motion climbing down the tree.*)
Through the swamp. (*Make fast motions, sliding hands.*)
Over the bridge. (*Thump chest.*)
Swim the brook. (*Make fast swimming motions.*)
Down the street. (*Tramp fast.*)
Ooooooh! or Wheeeew!

(*When children have shown that they can exercise control, they can stamp their feet as well as slap their thighs as they tramp.*)

VARIATION. At seasonal times, this may be a Witch Hunt, A Santa Claus Hunt, A Bunny Rabbit Hunt, and so forth. Use appropriate clues when you reach the cave.

Prayers Retarded children need to repeat quiet thoughts as well as verses which stimulate them and amuse them. They benefit from saying grace and prayers as normal children do.

Choose a simple grace and prayers written for young children of your faith; or use nonsectarian prayers. Say a line and have a child or group of children say it after you.

GRACE. Little children may use a one-line grace.

Thank you, God, for the food we eat.

More advanced children may say a verse, repeating line by line.

We bow our heads
And softly say,
"Thank you, God,
For our food today."

Many children like the Robert Louis Stevenson poem which starts, "Thank you for the world so sweet."

MORNING PRAYER. Start a work period at home or a school day with a prayer.

Dear God, we pray,
"Watch over us today;
Be with us while we work;
Be with us while we play.

EVENING PRAYER. End the day with a prayer.

Dear God, we say,
"Thank you for this day.
Be with us till we meet again,
For another happy day."

IV. Table Work and Games

A GENERATION OR SO AGO, A LARGE PART OF FAMILY LIFE CENTERED around the dining-room table. Almost every evening, especially in the winter, the family gathered in the dining room where Father read his paper, Mother mended, and the children did homework. Often, the family played simple games around this table. Admittedly, the scene is nostalgic, yet there is something solid about it, too. This doing different things together and playing certain games together did more to weld a feeling of belonging and to give each member of the family an understanding of his role in the group than any other family activity. Perhaps because of the repetition and routine of so many winter evenings, it remains one of the solid and satisfying memories of childhood; one feels warm and secure in remembering it.

This is the kind of acceptance and feeling of belonging that a retarded child must sense that he is receiving from his family and teacher if he is to feel secure; and he must feel this security before he can risk trying new things and learning new things.

A program of table work and games can be developed in a home as well as in a school. If carried on in a home, there should be a routine for days that are normally termed "school days." Each day set aside, at a certain hour, a period of time that is for work. This, in the beginning, may be as short as fifteen minutes and may be extended to an hour as ability increases. One family sets an alarm clock at 10 o'clock each morning. The retarded child shuts it off and knows that it is time for his work period to start. There is no need to be slavish in the routine. A picnic or an emergency could change the program. But children like to know that on a typical day certain things will happen at certain times.

Table work and games would literally include all activities which are done around a table. However, we have placed all activities which involve handicraft skills and making things under the two handicraft sections. The remaining activities fall into three areas, each of which contributes to development and learning in many ways.

There is the area of table activity that is fun! It involves the game technique. It is social in as much as it involves another person or persons.

There is the area that is solitary. At first a child must receive direction, but later he can work alone, developing his own interests. Many retarded children must eventually spend a great deal of time alone. They must learn how to occupy themselves.

There is another area that can be called work. All of the equipment that is used is sold in toy departments and adults would consider the activity play. But a retarded child needs work, mental work—not just more scouring pans. He needs it because everyone else has it. In as much as stringing beads in a pattern, matching numbers, sorting forms, and so forth, all require concentration and thought, it is well to call them work. Obviously, this work is not an end in itself, but a prelude to more advanced work involving the intellectual development of the child.

In this work period a teacher or parent should develop the work habit of completing a given task. It is a situation where a leader asks something of a child, where he places a responsibility to be fulfilled. It is here that a leader can develop attention span and insist, but only after he is sure that a child can do it, that one task be completed before another activity is started.

In this work period, you should develop a number of activities that initially require supervision and direction, activities which are on a level where the child can, with work, achieve successful performance. These activities should be repeated every day until a child can perform them with ease. The child should be completely familiar with the task at hand before a new task is added. As this work period progresses, occasionally repeat earlier activities that have been discontinued, as a review as well as keeping in mind the "cushion" activities principle. Needless to say this work period will contribute to independent or solitary activities.

A sample work period for a young retarded child who is just starting to have a work period might be: working with pegs, beads, puzzle, button strip, clay, clothespins, scribbling with crayons or pencil, and a simple matching and sorting activity.

When this kind of activity has been developed over a period of time, a teacher usually finds that he has more things to do than he has time to do them. This is a most satisfying point to reach. The teacher is now able to develop the ability to choose or select. When the required tasks have been completed, say, "Now, get something that you want to do." Granted that most decisions will be made for trainable children during their lives, they still need, in a limited way, to experience the right to choose when they can—for example, what song, what game, or what table activity.

This opportunity to choose cannot be offered until a variety of activities have been learned. You may be surprised to discover how often retarded children select the "cushion" activity, the one that is best known, the one which they feel most comfortable doing.

Warning. You must face the fact that sometimes, in spite of all your patience and all your time, a child does not seem able to learn to do a certain task which you feel he should be able to do. Don't be discouraged. Set the task aside. Try it at a later date. But ask yourself why it seems to be so difficult for him to learn what you are trying to teach. There may be a number of factors. He may not understand what you want him to do. He may not be ready physically to perform the task. He may be emotionally upset and unable to respond. He may not have had enough time to feel familiar with the preliminary or preceding tasks. He may fear failure. He may be tired. There may be no apparent reason.

It is hard to face failure in teaching. It is hard to ask questions. But by asking questions, by trying to view your child objectively, you will come to terms with your child's abilities and disabilities. When you discover what he can do, you can start there and work with him patiently, at his pace!

WORKING WITH PEGS

Fitting pegs into a pegboard is valuable exercise in eye-hand coordination and in manipulation to develop finger dexterity. It may also be used to develop interest span, to teach matching colors, and to teach the meaning of certain terms such as: *every* hole, row, outside rows, and so forth. A teacher, getting acquainted with a new child, may be able to roughly judge his attention span and his ability to complete a task by asking him to fill a pegboard with pegs. However, working with pegs is not a device to be used year after year (as it is in some places) just to keep a retarded child busy.

PEGBOARDS. There are several kinds of pegboards. Some have very large pegs and only a few holes to fill. These are useful for beginners. Other boards have more holes and pegs 1½ inches long; and others have tiny pegs with beads on top. The small pegs are the hardest to handle.

You can make a pegboard. Saw ¼-inch dowels into pegs. Bore holes, slightly larger than the pegs, all the way through a board, such as the end of an apple crate. Glue a piece of heavy cardboard on the bottom of the board. Color the pegs by dipping them in water tinted with food coloring.

EVERY HOLE. In the early stages, hand the pegs, one by one, to the child. This is especially helpful to a child who is easily distracted. Encourage the child to complete the entire board, but do not insist that he do so. Give him something else to do after a reasonable length of time. When you are certain that a child can complete the board, be firmer. Ask him to do the entire board, "Every hole!" Let him pick up the pegs himself. Later let him work without constant supervision.

67

Try to insert fun and imagination into this work period when you can do so without distracting the child. For example, when the pegboard is full, stand back and look at it saying, "Mmmmm! Looks like a birthday cake." Stop work to sing "Happy Birthday!" All children like the song, perhaps because one child becomes the center of attention. A child who has finished a board deserves attention.

Some children think the pegs look like matches and like to blow on them saying "Hot!" as they put them in the holes. This is good breath control exercise.

After a child has filled all the holes with pegs, ask him to put a bead over each peg. This requires more eye-hand co-ordination than putting a peg in a hole. When a child can fill the entire board with pegs with little prompting and in a reasonably short period of time, he is ready to do something different with pegs.

FENCE. The next task to ask a child is to build a fence with pegs, "just on the *outside*" of the board. Take h i s finger and move it along the outside row of holes on the board. Then place your finger, or his, in the center of the board and ask, "In here? No!" Move your finger to the outside row and ask, "Here?" Pause to see if he will nod or say, "Yes." If he  doesn't answer, you say, "Yes," nodding your head as you say it. If he has no speech, you may begin to establish communication in terms of "yes" and "no" while working with the pegboard. This may appear to be obvious, but actually it isn't, because it takes hundreds of experiences in a variety of ways to establish an understanding of yes and no. It takes even longer for a child to apprehend that he, too, can say "Yes" and "No."

This learning to make a fence may take awhile. To complete this task, a child has to remember, when he picks up a peg, that it goes *outside* and nowhere else. It takes thirty-six pegs to complete the fence on a standard board—and remembering something thirty-six times in a row is a big achievement!

So, if he gets a peg in the wrong place, don't show disapproval. Point to the peg that is out of place and say, "This peg doesn't belong here." Point to the outside row and say, "It belongs on the *outside*."

Sorting and Matching Colored Pegs A child can sort colors and match colors long before he can identify them, even mentally, by name. He doesn't have to think "blue" each time he adds a blue peg to a container holding other blue pegs. He depends upon visual discrimination.

Work with only two colors when you start to teach sorting and matching colors. For example, pick out the blue and red pegs and mix them up. Put a few blue pegs in a dish and say, "We are going to put blue pegs in this dish." Pick up a red peg and ask, "This kind? No!" Pick up a blue peg and ask, "This kind?" Pause to see if he responds. If he doesn't answer or nod his head, say, "Yes," nodding your head; and put the peg in the dish with the other blue pegs. Encourage him to pick up a peg and decide whether to put it in the dish or not.

When a child can sort out the pegs of one color, work with two pans. Put a few red pegs in one pan and a few blue pegs in the other. Hold up a peg and say, "Do we put this in this pan?" Wait for an answer. Supply it if necessary. Encourage him to hold up a peg and decide where to put it. When he has the idea of sorting and matching, he can work alone.

Add colors gradually, one at a time. Children often confuse purple with blue; so it is wise to eliminate the purple pegs for beginners.

ONE-COLOR FENCE. Now ask the child to make a fence on the

pegboard using only one color. Again, he does not need to know the name of the color. Pick up a blue peg and say, "We are going to make a blue fence." Put the peg in the pegboard on the outside row. Pick up a red peg and ask, "This kind?" Wait for a response as you did before.

When a child can make a fence with pegs of one color, give him a box containing beads of various colors. Ask him to sort the beads as he did the pegs, putting those of different colors in different pans.

MATCHING SHAPES. Now ask him to sort the beads according to shapes. Ask him to pick out the "blue beads that are round, like balls," or "blue beads that are square, like boxes."

If he has made a blue fence, ask him to put a blue bead that is round on top of each peg.

When a child has mastered all these tasks, the usefulness of the pegboard as a daily tool of instruction is over because the child has learned to pay attention, follow instructions, and to complete a task—very useful skills that can be utilized in learning other tasks. There are other activities that can be done with pegs, but the child has learned to do the basic ones.

Even though a pegboard is not used every day, it need not be abolished; it can become a "cushion" activity. A child may want to do the pegboard because he is comfortable doing it; he knows he can do it, and this knowledge gives him self-assurance.

After a child has learned a new task, ask him what he would like to do. At first he may seem lost and confused when asked to make a choice; but as he gains experiences, he will look forward to the moments when he can choose his activity. Often he will choose an early experience, like a pegboard which still remains an excellent exercise for eye-hand co-ordination and finger dexterity.

WORKING WITH BEADS

Stringing beads, like working with pegs, is an excellent eye-hand co-ordination and manipulation exercise which can be used in building other skills. It is much more difficult to string a bead than to place a peg at random into one of the many holes on a pegboard.

Use large beads. The round and square beads are more useful

than the egg-shaped and cylindrical ones. When a child has successfully filled a string with beads, praise him. Have some fun with the string of beads. Drape it around his neck and say, "Enough beads for an Indian chief!" Holler like an Indian. Or drape it around a girl's neck, saying, "What a lovely lady!" Imitate a grand lady. Ask a question about a party. Ask her where she got those "lovely beads." Or hold the string by one end, letting it swing like a pendulum saying, "Tick, tock! Hickory dock!" Rattle the beads when "the mouse ran down." End the verse with "Boo!"

MATCHING COLORS AND SHAPES. Put two beads of the same color on a string and say, "Will you please string yellow ones for me, just yellow." Pick up a blue one and ask, "This one? No!" Proceed as you did with pegs. Be sure that at different times the child strings all red, all blue, all green, all black, all yellow, and all orange. Many children confuse yellow and orange beads in this skill. If this happens, don't make an issue of it. Use other colors.

Next ask him to string colors alternately, for example: a yellow and a blue one; a yellow and a blue one. Do a few for a sample. Then string a square one and a round one, a square one and a round one.

COUNTING. When a child can string beads according to a pattern, start working with cards to develop counting, matching, and the beginning of sight vocabulary.

Begin with the same number of each color beads of the same shape. Draw the beads, on the card, making the figures the exact size and shape of the beads that the child will use. Color them with the colors to be reproduced on the string.

Write: 3 YELLOW 0 0 0
3 RED 0 0 0
3 BLUE 0 0 0
3 ORANGE 0 0 0

Draw the string between beads.

This card serves as a guide. Say to the child, "What color are we going to do first?"

The child either answers, "Yellow"; or, if he doesn't have speech the leader says, "Show me what we are going to do first." The child picks a yellow bead out of the box and shows it.

Then ask, "How many?" Whether the child has speech or not, you count, "one, two, three yellow." Be sure to count from left to right, touching each figure on the card.

When the child can make this pattern, try a more difficult combination; for example: three red, five yellow, three blue, five orange. Make a card, as you did before, as a guide.

In teaching this, say, "What color are we going to do first?" Point to the card. "Red. Let's count. One, two, three." Count as he strings the beads. Check with the card.

This is a hard exercise. Be patient. Don't be discouraged if a child can't do it for some time. Praise him warmly when he can do it by himself.

SORTING AND FITTING TOGETHER

There are many jobs done in sheltered workshops that basically involve the ability to sort and group. Certainly there are jobs around the house: setting the table; putting the silver and dishes away after they are dried; sorting clean laundry, especially socks; matching a button before sewing it on a shirt, and so forth.

In the beginning, you should have a quantity of several different types of sorting material so that you can be sure that the child understands what he is doing. As he sorts, you will be able to get some idea of his attention span and his ability to complete a job. At first, have him sort two types of things, like blue pegs and green pegs. He should be able gradually to increase his ability until he can sort five or six different things.

Here are a few of the many things which a child can sort:

Pegs according to color (page 69).

Beads according to color and also shape (page 70).

Change—either play or real money—pennies, nickles, dimes, and so on.

Figures on cards, sorting by form or color (page 73).

Swatches of plain material and figured material pasted on index cards.

Samples of different wallpaper pasted on index cards.

Dried lima beans and other soup beans.

SORTING BY SIZE. Sorting by size is an advanced sorting activity which requires judgment as well as visual discrimination. Cut out a number of circles, some big ones and some small ones. Ask him to put the big circles in one pile and the little circles in another pile.

Vary this activity. On another day, have him sort big and little squares. On a third day, give him big and little triangles, and so on.

Later mix the forms as well as the sizes and have him sort according to size and form. When he has finished his task, he will have a pile of big circles, a pile of little circles, a pile of big squares, a pile of little squares, and so forth.

Give him buttons to sort according to color, shape, and size. When a child has developed the ability to sort according to color, shape, and size, he has developed a considerable degree of visual discrimination and is ready to play some games and to fit things together.

Figures on Cards Being able to identify a figure pictured on a card, requires more ability than being able to identify a three-dimensional object which you can feel as well as see—such as a bead. Cut out a number of squares, triangles, circles, and stars large enough to fit on an index card without much space top or bottom. (It is hard for a child to distinguish between a rectangle and a square so do not use a rectangle—at least at first.)

If a child can color, have him color one or more a day. If he can't color, cut the forms out of construction paper, using blue, green, yellow, red, orange, and black. Don't try to teach a child the difference in shades. Paste the paper figures on index cards and use them for sorting.

Red Circle Take all the cards (above) which have circles of various colors on them. Place a shoe box (the pot) in the middle of the table. Deal the cards to the players. Players put the cards in front of them face up. The first player chooses a card and holds it up saying, "Red circle" (or whatever color circle is on the card). If he cannot talk, the leader says, "Red circle." Everyone is urged to look at the card, and then look at his cards to see if he has one like it. Players toss all the red circles that they have into the pot. The second player picks up a card and repeats the performance. The player who first gets all his cards in the pot wins. However, keep playing until all the cards are in the pot so that you have first winner, second winner, and so on.

Later play the game with other figures: stars, squares, triangles. Have children name them as above. When the children can play with all the forms, mix all the cards together. A card must match in color and form before it can be thrown into the pot.

Draw from the Pot Mix all the cards (page 73) with figures on them. Put a shoe box in the center of the table for a pot. Divide the cards into two equal piles. Put one pile in the pot. Deal the other pile to players. Players put their cards, face up, in front of them. A player draws a card from the pot. If he has a matching card, he puts the two matching cards in the "bank," that is face down next to him. If he does not have a matching card, he puts the card he drew in the "doghouse," slips it under the shoe-box pot. Play proceeds until someone has all his cards in his bank. If the pot is empty and there is no winner, take the cards out of the doghouse and put them back into the pot.

Other Cards When a child is familiar with geometrical shapes, make cards with other well-known forms on them. Color these only as you find them in nature. You might use: yellow pears, red and yellow apples, red, green, and yellow leaves, and flowers, Easter eggs, and butterflies in whatever colors you choose.

Use these cards for sorting and playing games as you did the geometrical figures (pages 73, 74). When a child can identify shapes like these and match their colors, he is ready for simple lotto-type games.

Lotto In playing lotto, a child learns to associate an object with a spoken word. He is able to make this association before he can say the word. His first step, in terms of the famed educator, Edouard Sequin, is to make the association of sensory perception with the name. The leader says, "This is a red circle," while displaying a red circle. The second step is recognition of an object by name. The leader says, "Show me the red circle." The third step is to remember the name which corresponds to the object. "What is this?" This piece of educational philosophy is important in teaching retarded children. They learn so slowly that a parent or teacher must give them experiences in the first type of learning before they are ready for another type. In playing lotto, you can progress from one type to the other without the child's knowing that there is any change in the game. There are many lotto games on the market, but you might do well to make a simpler one of your own.

I HAVE IT. This is a good family game as a retarded child has as much chance to win as another player if he is given time to match his cards. Make a master card for each player. Paste nine index cards containing forms on a shirt-cardboard, or other cardboard about that size and weight. Make sure that no form is duplicated on a card and that six colors are represented on each card: yellow, blue, green, red, orange, black.

Cards for five players might be:

1. Yellow star—black square—orange triangle—green Easter egg—blue circle—red leaf

2. Red star—orange square—green triangle—blue diamond—circle, half-red and half-black—yellow Easter egg

3. Yellow square—blue Easter egg—black diamond—green leaf—circle, half-orange and half-blue—orange star

4. Blue half circle—green apple—red Easter egg—yellow diamond—black triangle—circle, half-orange and half-green

5. Circle, half-orange and half-yellow—blue star—red diamond—yellow butterfly—green half circle—blackbird

Each player is given a cardboard with the forms on it. The leader has duplicate cards. He draws a card from his pile and says, "Who has a red circle?" (Or whatever he drew.) Each player looks at his cardboard. The player who has the red circle says, "I have it."

The leader asks, "What do you have?"

The child, if he can speak, answers, "A red circle." If he cannot speak, he indicates that he has it. The leader gives him the index card which he places on the identical picture on his cardboard. The first player to cover all the forms on his card wins.

75

This game may also be played with two people. The leader fills a card as well as calls.

When everyone has learned to associate the form with its name, the leader changes his method of asking. The leader shows a red circle and asks, "Who needs this?" When the child responds, the leader asks, "What is this?" The player answers.

When every player can identify the form without having the word spoken at the same time, the leader asks, "Who needs a red circle?" without showing the card. When a child responds, the leader asks, "Where do you need it?" The child points to the figure and receives the card.

PICTURE LOTTO. Using duplicate magazine or mail-order catalogues, make picture lotto cards and boards. You can group the pictures in many ways. You might have one game with pictures of things we eat; or things we wear; or things in the house, and so on. Play the game as I Have It, being sure to place emphasis on the association of the object and the spoken word.

If a child is having difficulty with a certain sound, or several sounds, include a number of pictures with words starting with this sound, but don't make him say it each time. For example, many children have trouble with "S." Have pictures of soap, soup, star, socks, and other "S" words mixed in with some other pictures.

NUMBER LOTTO. Cut large numbers from calendars and play as with other lotto games.

OTHER LOTTOS. You can make up games using words a child should learn, such as exit and go. Or use words in families like, bat, sat, rat. However, these games are advanced and most likely to be used with children ready to learn to read.

Fit Togethers Fitting things together requires visual discrimination, plus manipulation. You can use commercial toys which require a child to fit certain figures onto a matching peg or to drop a figure through a matching hole. There are small trucks and wagons which can be taken apart and put together again. You can also develop some table activities of your own which will help a child to fit things together.

JARS AND BOTTLES. Select a number of jars and bottles of different shapes and sizes, all with screw tops. Put them in a box. Take off all the tops. Leave the jars in the box. Put the tops on the table, all mixed up. Ask the child to put the correct tops on the correct bottles. Some children will try to do this hit and miss. Other children will try one top until they find a bottle that fits. Others will select one bottle and try every top on that. Others will use a certain amount of judgment, realizing that a big jar needs a big top.

This task requires eye-hand co-ordination, visual discrimination, plus muscular skill. After a child is familiar with the task, ask him to take off each lid. Put the bottles *in* the box and the lids *outside* the box. Then put the lids back on the bottles. Here are the concepts of on, off, in, and out. Plus two different kinds of twisting and turning.

NUTS AND BOLTS. Select different sizes of bolts with nuts that fit. Unscrew the bolts and ask the child to put them back on. A child can do this alone. If two children can do this well independently, select bolts of similar sizes and nuts to fit. Give each child an equal number of nuts and bolts. Let them race to see who can fit the nuts onto the bolts first.

TIN CANS. Carefully remove the tops of tin cans of graduated sizes, making sure that there are no rough edges. Have a frozen juice can, a soup can, a No. 2 can, and a No. 2½ can. Paint them yellow, red, blue, and green—or have the child paint them.

Turn the cans upside down and build a tower. Nest them together.

Trace around each can on one piece of cardboard. Color each circle the same color as the can that size. Have the child place each can on the matching circle.

BOXES. Choose boxes which can be nested together. Use only those with lids. Put a surprise in the smallest box. Have the child take

77

the boxes apart until he finds the surprise. If the surprise in non-perishable, like a doll or plastic animal, ask the child to put it inside the little box again and nest the boxes, fitting the correct lid on each one. There are many commercial toys of nested eggs, nested Indians, and so on, that have delighted all kinds of children for centuries.

GROUPING

So far, a child has been asked for the most part to match things that are identical. There has been some practice in finding things that are alike in some ways, but different in others. For example, he was asked to place a blue bead on a blue peg. He has had some experience in building up the concept that some things are bigger and some things are smaller than others. He must have realized this as he nested tin cans together or fitted tops on jars. It is now time to work on grouping.

In grouping, the objects may be different in many ways, but they have one thing in common. There may be a blue ball, a blue square, and a blue bird. The objects have color in common. There may be a red ball, a yellow ball, a green ball. The objects have form in common. Learning to group includes choosing which things are alike and eliminating the thing that is different.

It is easier to find which thing is different than which things are alike. Picking out the thing which is different involves choosing one thing. Finding two alike requires comparing two things. When a child selects the correct form that is different, ask him why it is different. If he can't tell you why it is different, explain it to him.

As a rule it is easier for a child to choose which thing is biggest or smallest than to choose two things which are alike.

There is a great deal of commercial material and games designed to develop seeing likenesses and differences, color recognition, and other basic skills. Much of this material is abstract or with so many details that it is confusing to the retarded child. It will probably be wiser to make your own materials, particularly for beginning activities. Remember successful achievement is the main goal, so begin simply.

Scrapbooks When a child can cut fairly well, he can make scrapbooks with pictures grouped in certain categories. One scrapbook might be pictures of things we eat; another, things we wear; another, things we ride, and so on. Other scrapbooks might be grouped according to rooms in the house. The kitchen scrapbook should include many kitchens to help a child to realize that kitchens do not have to look alike; yet they must be alike in certain ways. Each has a stove, sink, refrigerator, table, chairs, cupboards, and so forth.

Encourage a child to name the objects he sees in his scrapbooks. Encourage him to talk about each picture as a whole, if he will.

Which-One-Is-Different Cards Make a series of cards with four circles of identical size on each. On one card, color four of the circles red

and one yellow. On each of the other cards, color four of the circles one color, making one circle a different color. Use all the c o l o r s . Change the position of the odd circle.

Show the cards to the child, one at a time, having him name or point to the circle that is different. Let him hold the cards he gets right. Encourage him to tell you why the one circle is different.

Make another series of cards. This time use four identical forms and one odd form. All forms are the same color. For example, draw four green squares and one green triangle. Again show the cards to the child asking him to identify the form that is different. Let him hold each card that he identifies correctly.

A child wins the game if he gets all the cards. If more than one child is playing, the child with the most cards wins. Of course, there can be several ties if each card is identified correctly.

Which-Is-the-Biggest Cards Some children have difficulty in deciding which is the biggest and which is the smallest. Make a series of cards similar to those above. As the emphasis is on size, keep the color the same. For example, make a card with four circles the same size and color and one big circle the same color. Make another card with four circles the same size and color and one little circle. Use all the forms and the colors. Play and work with them as above.

Which-Two-Are-Alike Cards It is more difficult for a retarded child to see two forms that are alike than it is for him to identify a form that is different. Make a series of cards similar to those above and use them the same way. On one card, draw five identical forms; color two alike, and the others differently. For example: red circle, yellow circle, blue circle, and two green circles. Have the child point to the two that are alike and ask him why they are alike. If he cannot express himself, help him. Make more cards with other forms and other colors.

Make cards with forms that are different in shape, but the same in color—a red circle, red bird, red triangle, and two identical red apples.

Make cards with three figures that are different in color and form, and two figures that are alike but different in color—yellow star, green leaf, red circle, blue triangle, black triangle. Use other combinations and colors.

This is a difficult exercise. A child who can see that forms are alike in one way, although different in another, is ready for more advanced training.

Flannel Board You can use a flannel board to teach the preceding exercises on grouping. Use a commercial board or make your own. Cover a large piece of cardboard with flannel. Cut out the flannel shapes as above. When you press the flannel shape onto the flannel board, it stays in place.

You can also use cotton flannel which is less expensive. Cover the board with cotton flannel. Cut out construction paper forms. Paste a strip of cotton flannel on the back of each form.

CRAYONING

A retarded child needs a lot of experience and practice with crayons and pencils, repeated opportunities to scribble—make motions and marks back and forth, around and around, up and down —before he has the muscle control and the eye-hand co-ordination necessary to do any coloring that might in any way be termed handicraft.

However, if he is allowed to scribble too long without reason, he will sense that his efforts are aimless and will soon become bored. You can make very early efforts meaningful in a number of ways which involve both coloring and pasting.

Cut forms or objects to be colored out of strong paper. Place the form to be colored on a piece of newspaper. Ask the child to color it. He is not restricted in his movements as he goes back and forth, across the form and onto the newspaper. No one is standing over him, making him nervous, reminding him to stay within the lines.

Encourage him as he works saying, "Good! Put more red on it." Later say, "Color it so that I can't see any of the white paper." Don't be a perfectionist. When he is tired and he has colored the form to the best of his ability, have him rub paste on the back of it and paste it on a piece of contrasting or harmonizing construction paper with a "Bang! Bang!" as he pounds it with his fist. Make only one form a day, but add to the design from day to day. In this way, you are helping him to look forward, to plan, to make a project step by step.

The number of projects that can be done with this scribble effect are practically endless, especially if you add a line or two to complete a picture or ask a child to do it if he can.

A few suggestions are:

Easter. Eggs of different colors.

81

Spring. Flowers of different colors. Draw stems or cut some out of paper and paste them in place on the construction paper background. Have the child paste the flower on the stem.

Birds of different colors. Color an eye.

Butterflies of different colors. After they are pasted on paper, draw the antennae.

Kites of different colors. When they are pasted on paper, draw the tail, or past a piece of yarn under the kite for a tail.

Fall. Leaves of different colors. Draw veins with black crayon.

Christmas. Christmas balls of different shapes and colors. When they are pasted on paper, draw strings or hooks.

Christmas trees. Glue on ornaments or glitter.

Christmas stocking. Paste toys on top of stocking.

Christmas boot. Same as stocking.

Christmas candle. Color and paste the candle one day. Color and paste the flame the next.

Halloween. Pumpkins, cats and witches. Paste the cats and witches on colored chalk (page 101) or washpaint (page 105) background.

Thanksgiving. Various colored fruits and bowl or basket. Color the bowl or basket and paste it onto construction paper. Color the fruit day by day and paste it in the bowl or basket.

GREETING CARDS. Fold a piece of construction paper into fourths. Have a child color and paste one of the above forms on the outside. Write a message inside for him. Or cut a greeting from an old card and have him paste it on the inside.

WORK CARDS. Paste forms on in-

dex cards for sorting (pages 73, 74). Or make forms for number cards (page 91).

Color Pictures A child who is learning to stay within lines while coloring should have large pictures with little detail. Very few coloring books have suitable pictures. Sketch your own and save your patterns, adding to the collection each season.

Trace the picture onto coloring paper and outline it with heavy black crayon. If the picture needs some small detail, such as a few lines to indicate the wings of a duck, sketch these lines in with black crayon. Ask the child to color the picture. If the picture should have two colors, give the child color clues by marking each section with a little bit of the color he is to use. If the child has tried very hard to stay within the lines and still went outside frequently and appears to be upset by his failure, cut the picture out for him and let him paste it on construction paper.

Some common objects that are easy to color are:

A big apple with a stem and a leaf or two. Other fruits and vegetables.

A flower pot with formalized tulip and two leaves.

Hearts for valentines.

Baby chicks for Easter.

Clown and dolls with simple details.

Ice-cream cones.

Any of the pictures described in the first stages of coloring, only larger.

COLORING FOR OLDER CHILDREN. Older retarded children, who may need exactly the same practice in manipulating a crayon and staying within a line as younger children, may consider it more mature to color large numbers and letters while younger children are coloring balloons.

Your attitude while you are teaching these preliminary phases of coloring is extremely important. If you think that scribbling is babyish, the child will sense your feeling and never try to get beyond that stage. However, if you can make the child feel that what he is doing is interesting, and if you can make use of his work, he

83

will sense your approval and keep trying to do better. This is especially true of older retarded children with very young minds. Often the biggest problem a retarded child has to face is not his limitations, but other people's attitudes toward his limitations.

Geometrical Designs Children who have become familiar with geometrical figures while sorting and coloring cutout figures, may enjoy using them in designs.

GRANDMOTHER'S QUILT. Show the child a picture of a patchwork or "crazywork" quilt; or better yet, show him a quilt. Have him draw heavy black lines on paper, using a ruler. The lines may be squares and rectangles; or they may be lines drawn at many angles with large spaces in between.

Ask him to color the quilt. Encourage him to use different colors on touching squares.

PARQUETRY DESIGNS. He can do many things with parquetry designs, a combination of triangles and squares placed in design formations similar to those used in inlay flooring. Draw two identical squares on cardboard. Cut them out. Leave one square as it is. Cut the other in half diagonally, making two identical triangles. Place the forms in a pattern on drawing paper and trace around them. Outline the forms with heavy black crayon. Ask the child to color within the lines.

Trace around the forms again on paper, making a different pattern. Cut enough forms from construction paper to fit the forms on the drawing. Have the child paste the forms in the proper place.

Use a pattern as a puzzle. Cut two identical sets of forms from various colors of construction paper. Paste one set in a pattern on paper. Ask the child to fit the matching forms on top of those on paper. He can match form, color, and position.

CLAY WORK

A child needs a great deal of preliminary experience with plasticine, or similar modeling clays, before he can do anything that resembles handicraft. He can get a great deal of finger exercise and sensory pleasure as he squeezes it, pulls it, and makes it respond to his touch. However, he will need a lot of direction before he has learned to use it well enough to enjoy sitting down and making things by himself. Don't set a child at a table, give him a lump of clay, and tell him to play with it while you make cookies. You'll find squashed lumps of clay on the floor, table, and chair—a needless experience if you develop the project as work, something to be done with care.

Start by encouraging the child to make snakes, hamburgers, hot dogs, and pizza; all require rolling, squeezing, and patting clay. Then teach them to roll the clay with a dowel or rolling pin. Have him cut out shapes with cookie cutters or with little plastic molds that come with most dime-store sets of clay. Help him to make a basket and let him roll out a handle and pinch the clay together to hold it in place. He can make little eggs to fill the basket.

Have him make a long rope. Put a little lump of clay in the middle of the rope and say, "That's you, Timmy, sitting in a swing." Pick up the ends of the clay rope and sing, "Swinging in a Swing" (page 190). Have him do it.

When a child can handle the clay fairly well, there are two beginning methods for using it.

PUSH AND PULL. The child has one lump of clay which he pushes, pinches, and squeezes into an object. For example, he wants to make a pig. He has a round lump of clay. He squeezes it into an oval, the general shape of the body. Then he pinches it to shape the head and the legs and a little tiny tail.

COMBINING PARTS. The child has a number of small lumps of clay which he shapes by pushing, pulling, pinching and rolling between his palms. He presses these parts together to make various objects. For example, he makes three balls for a snowman and pinches them together. He may make a boy, cat, almost anything, this way.

When the work period is over, have the child put the clay in a can with a cover where it will stay moist.

WORKING PUZZLES

Working puzzles requires many types of learning and develops finger dexterity as well. Once a retarded child has learned the technique, he usually loves to do puzzles, old ones and new ones, and enjoys working alone.

When you begin to teach a child to use puzzles, use the wood-inlay type, bounded by a frame with a backing, with no more than five to nine pieces. Use two types: one in which each inlay piece is a complete figure in itself; another in which a single inlay figure is divided into pieces to be fitted together in the frame.

Look at the picture in the frame and talk about it. Ask the child what it is. If he cannot talk, say, "Look at the funny duck." Empty the pieces on the table and ask the child to put the puzzle together again. If he does not respond, begin by putting a piece in place saying, "See." Take the piece out and say, "Now, you do it." Guide his hand if necessary. Praise him for his effort, even if you can't praise him for achievement.

The child should develop some understanding of at least three simple directions before he can advance with working puzzles.

1. "Turn it over." When he has a piece upside down, pantomime turning it over as you speak. If he doesn't understand, demonstrate as you speak and then ask him to do it. If he still doesn't comply, do it for him.

2. "Move it around." When he has a piece in the right area, but wrong position, rotate your finger over the area advising him to move it around. If he doesn't comply, rotate the piece and if necessary place it in the place saying, "See it fits. Now you do it." Guide his hand if he can't do it.

3. "It won't fit." When he has the piece over the wrong area, point to the correct area and say, "Try it here." If he doesn't comply, do it yourself saying, "See it fits."

When the picture has been put together again, with or without help, pause and look at it. Talk about it. Make the child feel that you think it is fun to put a puzzle together.

When a child has learned to do a simple puzzle independently, give him a slightly more difficult one—one with more pieces. As days pass, give him more puzzles, gradually increasing the difficulty and at the same time allow him to "review" his old ones. Eventually give him an inexpensive cardboard puzzle which also has a frame and backing.

Never minimize a child's achievement even if it appears to you that he has learned each puzzle by rote. If you observe him carefully, you will discover that he is advancing in his method of working from a completely trial and error system to a system using color clues and form clues—plus trial and error.

FOLLOWING DIRECTIONS. Working with puzzles offers an excellent opportunity to teach a child to follow directions and obey commands. This training is perhaps the most useful you can give him.

When the puzzle is complete, ask the child to put the "Duck puzzle" away. If necessary, point to the place where it should go. When it is time to do puzzles again, ask him to get the "Duck puzzle." When he can obey your commands without your pointing and at an unexpected time in the day, you can be sure that he understands your speech—even if he has no speech of his own. He has reached a significant point.

In this speech training, remember that a child must hear a great deal of speech before he can reproduce it. This does not mean that adults around him should talk a lot. It does mean, however, that you should make a point of naming objects with which a child is working. Speak in a clear, unhurried manner with a well modulated voice so that he can build up the meaning of words. Give your commands in the same fashion. Show approval when a child obeys.

Homemade Puzzles A child may like to make his own puzzles. Paste a colorful picture on a shirt cardboard. Cut it into pieces to be assembled as a puzzle. Make each piece large. Cut only on straight lines.

SELF-HELP PRACTICE

Learning self-help skills, such as buttoning things together, can be just as much a part of table work as working puzzles or matching cards.

To make a simple button strip for beginners, take two pieces of quilted material, 4 inches by 12 inches. Cut five slits, evenly spaced, that are wider than the large buttons you are going to use. Overcast the edges with red yarn or thread, or any other bright color. Firmly sew five different large buttons, evenly spaced, on the other piece of material so that they lie directly beneath the buttonholes when the two pieces of material are placed one on top of the other. Machine stitch the two pieces together like an envelope, leaving one long side open.

SURPRISE BUTTON BOARD. A child has to unbotton the buttons on a surprise button board in order to see the picture which is inside. He should then rebutton the material.

To make a surprise button board, paste an interesting picture, such as a pet, on a piece of smooth wood about 8 inches by 12 inches. Attach strips of material to either side of the board, one with buttons, the other with buttonholes. These strips should be wider than the board so that when they are buttoned a child can slip his hand under the cloth to manipulate the buttons.

If you plan to use this board for some time, make a changing-picture board. Cut the flap from a heavy envelope about the size of the board. Cut out the center, leaving a wide margin. Slip a different picture into the envelope each time you plan to have the child work with the board.

OLD VEST BUTTON STRIP. Make a more difficult button strip for an old vest. Cut a strip about 3 inches wide from either side of the vest. Sew these to a flat piece of material about 4½ inches wide and as long as the strips.

ZIPPER BOARD. Make a zipper board like the button boards. Use the heavy type zipper such as is used on jackets. The ends have to be fitted together before it will zip.

Other Fasteners Retarded children must learn how to buckle belts and straps. Give a child a belt or a buckle and teach him to manipulate it as he holds it in front of him where he can see it. Later he can learn to buckle a belt or strap on clothes he is wearing.

A child also needs to learn to fasten a hook and eye, especially the large kind that is found on boys' pants. Again let him work with a hook and eye on a strip which he can hold in front of him. Later he can learn to fasten his own garments.

Lacing a Shoe Lacing involves the skill of putting a lace in a hole and pulling it out. Lacing a shoe also requires working with two strings and going from side to side. When working at a table, use a real shoe with the toe pointed away from the child. This position is similar to a shoe on a foot.

It is helpful to use two shoe laces, white and black, tied together and of equal length. Put these through the bottom two holes of the shoe and tie them so that they can't slip through the holes. As you work with the child, emphasize "first white one then black one," "over and under," and so on. When he can do this well with the two laces of different colors, have him work with one shoe lace.

Tying a Bow Tying a bow is extremely difficult for most young retarded children. Many of them are not ready to learn this important skill; yet, most of them want to learn to do it. Be patient as you help the child who wants to learn; work with him step by step. Praise him when he can do step one and two; help him if necessary with step three and four. Make him feel that someday he is going to learn to tie a bow all by himself.

Most people who successfully teach this skill seem to develop an individual way of teaching it that works for them and often doesn't work for other people. A few tips on methods that have been used and an analysis of the steps involved may help you get started. Then you too will work out a way to teach a child how to tie a bow.

When you begin to teach a child to tie a bow, use Venetian blind cord, clothesline rope, or wide ribbon. We have had best results in two ways: 1. At a table with the child tying the cord around a long shallow box placed flat on the table. The leader stands beside or in back of the child to direct the procedure. 2. With the child standing and tying the cord around a large roll of paper which is standing upright or around a pole.

There are four steps involved in tying.

1. Take the two ends of the cord, one in each hand, and put one end over and under the other. Pull the ends.

2. Make a loop near the knot.

3. Go over your thumb that is holding the loop and over and under the loop.

4. (And this is the difficult one!) Put your finger under the cord that is not part of the loop. Push it against your thumb that is holding the loop. Push your thumb out of the way and push the cord into the opening that is left. You now have two loops. Grasp them and pull them.

When a child can tie a bow with big cord, gradually reduce the size of the material until he can tie a bow with a shoelace and string.

NUMBER WORK

A retarded child likes to count. It makes him feel like other children who are always number conscious. "We have three cars." "We have five bathrooms." "I ate sixty pancakes," normal children will say as they play. The retarded child doesn't have any concept of what the numbers mean (and neither do a lot of normal children who are doing the talking) ; but the retarded child has the idea that numbers are important; and, of course, they are.

Parents should not try to develop academic school work with a retarded child, but they can help a great deal by presenting experiences that will help the child to develop a concept of numbers that will be helpful in everyday life and lay a foundation for more formal training—if the child has the latent ability to advance to a certain degree.

A child may learn to count by rote long before he has any understanding of numbers. He may be able to say "1, 2, 3" before he can hand you three beads or follow your instructions to take two cookies. He likes the rhythm of counting, and goes through a period when he never seems to tire of counting the fingers on his hand, 1, 2, 3, 4,

5—with a long drawn out *five,* and perhaps a clap of the hands and "Good!" if he said it correctly. He loves counting songs and chants like, "One, two, buckle my shoe," and so forth.

Encourage a child to count with you—three drawers in the dresser as you put away the socks, 1, 2, 3; six cookies on a plate, 1, 2 ,3, 4, 5, 6. Ask him to bring you two pencils or one chair. Look for opportunities to build up his liking for and his awareness of numbers and then create an understanding of them.

A child will be able to arrange written figures in sequence before he really knows the difference between them. You can do a great deal to help him to understand the relationship between a spoken number, a written number, and objects for which they stand. Keep each number work period short.

Roll the Cubes Pick up six cubes and roll them on the table like dice. Ask, "How many?" The child or children count them. Roll the cubes again, a different number this time. The child or children count them, 1, 2, 3, 4.

Ask the children to close their eyes and open them when they hear the cubes land on the table. Don't forget to roll none! Children should learn that sometimes there are none.

Picture Cards Make a series of cards with groups of pictures pasted on standard sheets of construction paper. On each piece of paper have a group of pictures cut from magazines representing a certain number. For example, have three dogs, three hats, three girls. Avoid pictures with distracting details. Six similar objects is a high enough quantity in this early procedure.

Mix the cards up. Show a card. Ask, "How many dogs?" If the child doesn't answer or try to count, say, "Let's count." Touch each figure from left to right and count, "1, 2, 3."

Number Cards Make a set of cards with individual numbers on them —one through twelve. Make another set having identical form and color but a different number of forms on each: one black circle on one card, two black circles on another card, and so forth, through twelve. Place the figures in a row. Encourage a child to count them from left to right.

Take the number cards. Give the child a card and ask him to find the number like it on the clock or on a calendar.

Place the cards in sequence. Then mix them up and ask a child to place them in order. Repeat this until it is well done.

Take a card with circles and say, "How many? Let's count. 1, 2, 3. Where is number three?" If he can point to number three on the set of number cards, fine. If he can't say, "Let's count. 1, 2, 3. Here it is!"

Then say, "Let's put three circles on top of number three." As the child develops ability, add number cards and form cards up to twelve. With this amount of recognition skill a child can dial a telephone from a written number, find a street address, have some concept of time in relationship to the clock, possibly measure even inches, and do some household chores which involve simple number work.

Shuffle the number cards. Have the child arrange them in sequence. Shuffle the form cards. Have the child arrange them in sequence. If he can do these tasks, he is ready to learn some simple arithmetic.

Stoop Cards A variation of this activity (above) is stoop cards, which requires a child to use large muscles as he stoops to put cards on the floor. Make large cards, 8 inches by 12 inches, similar to the ones above. Make a large paper clock. Place the hands on 1. The child finds card 1 and lays it on the floor. He turns the hands of the paper clock to 2, and lays card 2 next to 1, and so on.

He can place the cards with forms on top of those with numbers as he did with small cards.

Calendar Matching Paste two sheets from the same old calendar on durable paper. Leave one sheet as it is. Cut the other sheet into squares with one number on a square. Mix the squares. Ask the child to put each square on the corresponding number on the calendar.

Trace and Color Give a child a simple form, like an egg or an apple. Give him a sheet of paper with a number written in the corner. Ask him to trace around the form, drawing six eggs or three apples, or whatever the number indicates. Ask him to color the forms.

If you have a class, each child can draw a number picture. Place them on display in order.

Number Skip An advanced retarded child may enjoy filling in blanks with missing numbers. Paste odd numbers from a calendar on a sheet of paper, leaving blanks for the even numbers. The child fills in the missing even numbers with figures cut from the same calendar. Make another set, pasting the even numbers on the card and asking the child to fill in the odd numbers.

V. Learning Handicraft Skills

ALTHOUGH RETARDED CHILDREN ARE NOT CREATIVE IN THE GENERAL sense of the word, they love handicraft because it satisfies a number of their needs in a special way. In the first place, a child can see the results of his efforts, and this to a person who is constantly frustrated, means a great deal. When a child picks up a crayon and makes a long thick mark on a sheet of paper, he can see his mark. If he lacks speech and imagination, his mother may say, "I see a road, a winding road." Chances are the child will make more winding roads, or perhaps unmeaningful lines. But he need not stop there. One of the big advantages of handicraft work is that it can start very simply, but it has no limits. It is also an activity which a child can enjoy when he is very young, and also enjoy when he is old. He can enjoy it at home or at school. Retarded children, who have been trained over a long period of time, do produce some really lovely handicraft products.

FEELING OF ACHIEVEMENT. The act of producing something of his own gives a child a feeling of confidence and achievement. The parent, or teacher, who is guiding him must, therefore, be especially sensitive to the child's ability, judging carefully what the child can do and what he cannot do, deciding when to help him and when not to help, in order that this experience in art will bring a feeling of confidence and achievement and not added frustration. Very frequently a parent or teacher may wish to prepare part of a project in advance, such as punching holes in an article for lacing, and allow the child to finish it—often with help. If the child has put sufficient time and effort into the product, he will still feel that it is his.

CO-ORDINATING INTERESTS. Handicraft blends with other activities and helps a child to feel that he is living an integrated life. Any interest—play activities, changing seasons, and so forth—may be reflected in handicraft. A snowflake on a window pane may prompt one to show a child how to cut a paper snowflake. A class visit to a farm may be followed by coloring pictures of farm animals. Any imaginative parent or teacher can integrate handicraft with daily experiences or learning activities. Handicraft may also be done just for fun.

SPEECH AND SOCIAL DEVELOPMENT. Art work and handicraft almost always give rise to conversation. A parent need not rave about a few scribbled lines, but he can truthfully say. "That's red. I like red." Of course, when a child does do something well, he should receive praise; and he loves it. A child should be encouraged to talk about his own work, and often he will.

A child often wants to give his handicraft work to someone or he wants the entire family to enjoy the favors which he has made for the table or the decoration for a holiday. Handicraft gives a child the chance to contribute to the joy of others—an outlet that we all need but one which a retarded child often misses because it is hard for him to find ways that he can give to others.

Through care of equipment, a child may learn to be orderly and may practice the self-discipline of picking up when he has finished a task. Like any child, he may need reminding and sometimes help.

PHYSICAL AND SENSE DEVELOPMENT. A child's senses of touch and smell and his concepts of different materials can be quickened as he works with different handicraft materials. He can he helped to realize that wood is hard and firm; paper and cloth are flexible; paint is runny; paste is gooey and sticky; clay is punchy; paper is

95

smooth; cotton flannel, felt, and velvet are soft, and so forth. Some-things have smells. Others don't.

Many retarded children develop a sense of color which goes be-yond mere identification of colors. They may develop a sense of pattern and even rhythm in art work. They may sense what is pleasing to look at and what is not.

Certain art and handicraft work, such as finger painting, paint-ing with a large brush, hammering, and modeling with clay, pro-vides a release from tension. Making big swoops with a paint brush or a hand or arm, pounding nails, punching clay are all controlled outlets for pent-up energies and harbored feelings.

In working with materials, cutting, pasting, folding, painting, and so forth, a child develops muscles, especially small muscles which might not otherwise be used, he develops eye-hand co-ordination, and he develops skill in handling equipment. Many of these skills, basic as they are, are the very ones that he will need if he ever has a chance to work in a sheltered workshop or a very protected indus-try, pasting on labels, gluing insignia on cowboy hats, folding hand-bills, or any of other such activities. A retarded child needs to repeat and repeat a skill and should be given as many different ways to use each skill as possible. He should be encouraged to combine his skills. Many handicraft projects require a person to cut, paint, fold, and paste in the process of making an article. A child should be encour-aged at all times to advance as best he can. He should also be en-couraged to repeat the things which he likes to do and does well.

WORK PLACE. If possible, have a regular place to do arts and crafts work. There should be a place for everything and everything should be in its place after each work period. It is a very good idea to label each container with the printed word and, when possible, with a picture of the article—mail-order catalogues have pictures of almost everything. If a child has trouble carrying a box filled with small objects, put them in a pail. It is easier to carry a pail than a box be-cause a pail may be grasped with one hand; and as one walks, a certain amount of sway is permissible. A box must be carried with two hands and held steadily. Crayons, for example, may be kept in a small sand pail. Paper should be kept in a box with a lid, where it will stay clean and neatly piled. Entire sheets of paper may be kept in one box, scraps of construction paper in another. A child should be taught not to waste. If you have more than one pair of blunt scissors, they should be kept together. Have everything ready before you begin a session—table covered, equipment and material on hand, a sample or pre-cut portion of the work ready to use. If too much time and effort is spent getting ready to work, there will be no time or energy left for the project itself. Work in an unhurried atmosphere and an uncluttered place. Believe that the thing that the child is going to make is important. Be willing, at first at least, to give the project your time and undivided attention.

INTEREST SPAN. Interest span in art or handicraft work may at first be very short, but it usually increases. It is worth-while to get out materials and equipment for a few minutes' work.

Children like, at first, to draw, paint, or make things that are quickly finished in one sitting. Later they may enjoy planning something that will take more than one day. For example, they may start a paper chain, work on it a few minutes, put it away, and then make it longer the next day. Or a child may make a picture. On the first day, the child is given a piece of paper with a line on it. He is told that he is going to make a picture with sky, grass, and a tree. He paints blue sky above the line. The next day, he paints green grass below the line. The third day he pastes a pre-cut picture of a tree on the grass, with the sky as a background. Concepts such as learning to plan, in a limited way, and looking forward to doing something the next day do have a transfer from one aspect of life to another.

After a child has learned to like to paint, paste, cut, and so forth, has increased his interest span, and has developed his skills, he may be able to work for a considerable period of time by himself. He will still appreciate interest in his work, but a mother or teacher does not need to give him undivided attention while he is working. Of course, handicraft work does not have to be limited to pasting and coloring and making little odds and ends. Many children eventually learn to knit, weave on simple looms, braid rugs, embroider, and do simple woodwork. In later life, they derive great satisfaction following these handicraft hobbies during their leisure time.

PRESENTATION. In the following pages we have described methods

97

used in teaching skills to retarded children with varying degrees of mental and physical ability. Following each description are projects designed to allow children to use these skills. Most projects require more than one skill—for example, cutting and pasting. This is as it should be because no one should be allowed to forget one skill while learning another; and in life, most work and play represent a combination of skills.

In describing the projects, we have not tried to decide what the child can do and what should be prepared in advance or what help should be given. The situation varies with almost every child and most certainly with every class. In a few cases, we have suggested the manner in which a project has been successfully presented, hoping that a teacher or parent may profit from another's experience. At other times we have suggested using pre-cut material because we wished to place emphasis on some skill other than cutting and felt that a child might tire of the entire project if he should spend too much time on a preliminary phase of it.

It should go without saying that before an adult attempts to teach any handicraft he must first understand directions himself and be able to make a project without referring to the book. It is often a good idea to make a sample, show it to a child, and say, "We are going to make this." The fact that an adult made the project, and thinks that the child can make it, gives the child confidence. It also gives an adult confidence in teaching.

PLAYING WITH COLOR

Obviously, there is a great deal of muscular eye-hand co-ordination wielding a paint brush or in grasping and coloring with a crayon, and a lot of observing of relationships when a child paints grass green and sky blue. However, these are not the chief reasons for giving retarded children experience with paint and color. There are many things in the experience itself that go far beyond the finished project.

Everyone is intrigued with what paint will do. It brightens a room or "tones" it down. Colors run together, or can be mixed, to form unlimited shades. People react to color, often unconsciously, as some colors are soothing and cool, and other colors are stimulating and warm. Most children, including mentally retarded children, gain their first concept of "pretty" while playing with color.

Let the child get the idea of color before he starts to draw or paint something. Before trying anything with a brush, initiate sponge, stick, and potato printing (page below, 100) which give the idea of transfer of color from one place to another. Follow with finger, string, and comb painting (pages 101, 102, 104, 136, 138) which give rhythmic movement with paint. Crayoning (pages 81-84), and "free" painting all give experience with color.

In the following projects only material, not equipment, is listed. For example, if paper is held in place with paper clips which are removed when project is finished it is not included. Crayons, pencils, and so forth are included as part stays on paper.

SMOCK. *Materials:* man's worn shirt, plastic cloth about 12 inches wide and 24 inches long, thread or staples

Make an artist's smock from an old shirt and encourage a child to wear it any time that he is working with paints. Cut off the collar and cut the sleeves off at the child's elbow. Cut a piece of plastic cloth, or other water-proof material, about 12 inches wide and almost as long as the shirt. Staple or sew this piece of material inside the back of the shirt. The child wears the shirt backward, with one or two buttons buttoned down the back. The plastic strip helps to keep his front dry.

Decorative Printing You can decorate paper and use it for a number of purposes: as gift-wrapping paper, covers for scrapbooks, to decorate a waste basket, pencil holder (page 149), or other containers, or placemats. Try to find some use for everything that a child makes.

PRINTING PAD. Cut pieces of felt, pieces of blotting paper without shiny backs, or pieces of newspaper to fit into the bottom of a paint pan or saucer. Put the pieces on top of each other to make a pad about 1/4 inch thick. Pour poster paint on it until the pad is saturated, but not floating in paint. As the pad becomes dry, add more paint.

SPONGE PRINTING. *Materials:* poster paint on pad (above), paper to be decorated

Cut synthetic sponge into 1 or 1 1/2 inch cubes. Moisten the sponge.

99

The child presses the sponge on the printing pad and then dabs here and there on the paper. When the sponge is without color, he again presses it on the pad and continues to decorate the paper until he has colored it to his satisfaction.

He can use one color, or a combination of colors. For example: Christmas paper may be green and red; Easter paper, purple and yellow; Halloween paper, orange and black—or any other combination.

STICK PRINTING. *Materials:* poster paint on pad (above), paper to be decorated

Almost anything may be used for a printing stick: spools; dowels; small sticks—like lath—; small tumblers; or pieces of felt cut into rectangles, squares, triangles or other shapes and glued to the end of spools; or string glued in swirled forms to the end of spools.

The child presses the stick or form onto the printing pad and then dabs here and there on the paper. It may be hit or miss fashion, or in a pattern. He can use one form, or a combination of forms; one color or a combination of colors.

An advanced child can produce a formalized effect. Fold the paper into sections. Open it. Stamp a form within each section. Or crease the paper. Stamp above the crease and below the crease.

POTATO BLOCK PRINTING. *Materials:* poster paint, paper

Cut a potato in half horizontally and blot cut surface on newspaper.

Cut a silhouette form from cardboard which will fit onto the cut surface of the potato. It should be a simple form with clear-cut angles —such as a bell or tree at Christmas time, a tulip, a jack-o'-lantern, or a heart. Place the form on the potato and draw around it. Cut down around the outline with a sharp knife. Cut in from the side about ½ inch until the knife meets the vertical cut. Remove the unwanted parts of the potato. Use a pen point

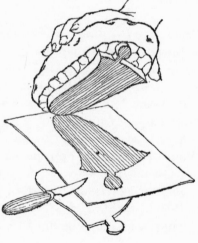

100

in reverse to gauge out small sections, such as eyes. Put a small amount of paint in a flat dish.

The child presses the prepared potato into the paint, then presses the print carefully onto the paper. He dips the potato into the paint before each print.

He can print paper hit and miss for wrapping paper. Or he can decorate a strip, such as a strip of hearts, and hang it over a door. Or he can make valentines, Christmas cards, or other greeting cards decorated with potato prints.

Wet-Chalk Drawing

Materials: paper, water, chalk

Wet-chalk drawings look like pastel paintings when dry.

The child wets a piece of paper with a sponge. He colors the sky and grass, using the side of a piece of chalk, and then completes the scene, drawing a tree, house, or other large object—again using the side of the chalk.

VARIATION. *Additional materials:* pre-cut picture, paste

After the child has colored the sky and grass, let the paper dry. Later have him paste a pre-cut picture on the background.

String Painting

Materials: poster paint, paper

Put small amounts of different, but harmonizing, shades of paint in two or three small paint pans or saucers. Give child a heavy piece of string about 12 inches long. He dips the string into some paint and "snakes" or swirls it across the paper. He dips the string into another color of paint and swirls it across the paper. He may use the same string for all colors or he may use a string for each color. You can use this painting as decorated paper (page 99). You will get a different effect if you use Folded Paper String Painting (page 138).

PORTFOLIO. *Materials:* paint, shirt cardboards

Decorate two cardboards which the laundry inserts in ironed shirts —or pieces of cardboard about that size. Punch holes at regular intervals around three edges. Lace the two pieces of cardboard together to make a portfolio to hold pictures and other "work."

Finger Painting Finger painting is an acceptable messy activity which can be therapeutic, as well as fun. It produces a sensory satisfaction that is tension relieving, in a way similar to water play, sand-box play, making mud pies, and working with clay and gooey papier-mâché.

However, even though we recognize its values in terms of manipulation and tension relieving, finger painting will interest a child more if we do something with it. Most retarded children will not produce recognizable finger-print pictures. We must use their paintings as decorated paper (see page 99).

RECIPE. *Materials:* lump starch, water, soap flakes, poster paint or food coloring

Finger paint is expensive to buy and is comparatively simple to make. Dissolve one cup of lump starch in a little cold water. Add one quart of boiling water and boil until thick. Remove from the range and beat in with a spoon one cup of white soap flakes (not powder). Cool thoroughly. Divide into four or five jars. Add one teaspoon or a little more of poster paint to each jar. Or add enough food coloring to get the shade you wish. Yellow and orange are not always effective. If you do not like the shades you get, you may buy these two colors.

PROCEDURE. *Materials:* glazed paper (shelving paper or glazed wrapping paper), finger paints (above), water

Cover the workspace with newspaper or plastic cloth. Place a large piece of glazed paper, shiny side up, on the newspaper or plastic cloth. Wet the paper thoroughly with a cloth or sponge. The child spreads the water evenly with his hands, pushing off the excess.

Put a teaspoon of paint in the center of the paper and encourage the child to push it around, but not off the paper. This is the time to talk about the different parts of the hand. "Let's see what they will do."

1. Use the whole hand, flat and relaxed. Push the paint around.
2. Make a fist, thumb up. Pound, pound, here and there.
3. Use the side of the hand, fingers held straight. Make lines this way and that.
4. Try your finger tips. Make them squirm through the paint.
5. Use one finger or thumb.
6. Make a fist. Rotate your wrist, round and round in the paint.

7. Scratch with your fingernails, lightly and softly.

8. Make a fist. Use your knuckles. Rotate lightly and softly.

9. If the child is advanced, see what he can do with his whole arm and elbow.

If the paint tends to dry, add a few drops of water. When the child has discovered what his hand will do, experiment with color by putting a small amount of another color of paint on the background color in various places—such as red on blue which will give violet tones; blue on green which will give aqua tones: yellow on red which will give orange tones, and so on. You may later place some of the blending colors on separate pieces of paper. The child dips his finger or fist into this and applies it.

When the child has finished painting, wipe his hands with a large wet cloth to remove the paint. Rinse the cloth in a pail of water.

The finger painting should be pressed. Cover your ironing board with brown paper. When the finger painting is dry, lay it on the ironing board with the painting next to the brown paper. Press it with a warm iron.

HANDPRINTS. While the child's hand is still covered with paint, take a piece of clean drawing paper and ask the child to hold his fingers open and to press his hand on the clean paper to make a print. If you are working with a group, have each child make a handprint. When the prints are dry, exhibit them. See if the children can identify the hands.

FOOTPRINTS. If you are working out-of-doors, you may enjoy making a footprint. When the paper is full of paint, lay it on the ground. Have the child step on the paper with one foot and then press the foot on a clean sheet of paper to make a print. Wipe the foot dry, return finger painting to table, continue using the hand to make a finger painting.

FINGER-PAINT PRINTS. When the child has produced an interesting design, ask him to stop. Place a piece of ordinary paper or drawing paper on the finger painting. Rub it lightly. Lift it. See what happens!

Encourage the child to go on painting, perhaps adding a different color. When the design is interesting, ask him to stop again.

Make another print. See the difference. These prints may look something like block printing. They do not need to be ironed like the original finger painting.

Comb Painting

Materials: cardboard, poster paint, paper to be decorated

Make a cardboard comb from a piece of medium-weight cardboard a b o u t 2½ inches square. The comb must not be wider than the pan which will hold the paint. Cut notches along one edge of the cardboard, making sure that the bottom of t h e "teeth" are kept flat. The depth of the notches may vary from ½ inch to 1 inch and the width of each notch may vary from ¼ inch to ½ inch.

Experiment with the comb by using water on a blackboard. Pour a little water in a small paint pan or saucer. Dip the comb in the water.

Show the child what you can do with it. Let him imitate each of your movements. Make the comb wiggle up and down across the blackboard; zig-zag up and down, go around and around. Use straight strokes in all directions. Make dots. See how each stroke makes a different design.

Now, use paint instead of water in the paint pan. Again, show the child and let him imitate you. Make designs on the classified ad section of a newspaper. When the child understands what he can do, let him choose what kind of strokes to make. Then let him work on white or colored construction paper. He can combine comb-painted designs with stick designs (page 100). Use the paper to wrap gifts or in making useful articles.

Painting In finger painting, we saw what the hand can do. Now, let's see what the brush can do! Start by painting with water on a black-board. Make the brush wiggle, going up and down across the black-board; zig-zag, going up and down, go around and around, go halfway around. Use straight strokes in all directions, or in one direction. Make dots by dab-dabbing here and there.

After seeing what the brush can do, experiment with free paint-ing. Let the child paint anything he wants to paint on paper. Use a household paint bush, 1 or 1½ inches across. See what he can do with a smaller paint brush. Experiment with Stained Glass Windows (page 133), Crayon and Paint Picture (page 137), and Scrape Away Picture (page 136). All of these different techniques give a child experience with color.

Wash-Background Pictures
Materials: paper, paints, pre-cut picture

The child paints the background for a picture, using strokes go-ing straight across a paper. He paints a sky above and grass below. When the paint is dry, he pastes a pre-cut picture of a tree, house, or any other object on the background. Or he can paint a sea and a sky at sunset; and when the paint is dry, paste a picture of a sailboat on the sea. Or he can paint a sky on a "scary" Halloween night with red and yellow running together, and perhaps a little purple at the top or bottom of the picture; and when the paint is dry, paste on a pre-cut picture of a witch riding broomstick.

Crayoning A child may wish to experiment with crayoning as he did with painting, making free marks on paper to get the "feel" of the crayon, to learn to color only on the paper, and to see what happens when he makes marks with different **colors**. He should not be given coloring books or pictures to color until he has learned the meaning

105

of staying inside or outside lines, and has developed the ability to do so (pages 81-84).

Picture Frame

Materials: paper, crayon, pre-cut picture, paste

One of the best ways to teach a child the meaning of coloring within a certain area is to have him make a frame for a pre-cut picture.

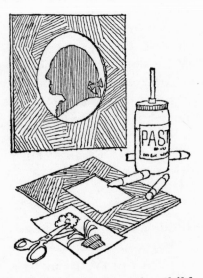

Show him a sample which he will think is pretty and wish to copy. Have the pre-cut picture as well as other materials on hand. Talk about what you are going to do.

With a heavy black crayon, draw a straight line about 1 inch in from the edges of the paper. Explain. "We are going to color a picture frame first. Then we shall paste the picture inside the frame. The picture frame is *here.*" Take the child's finger in your hand and run it over the space to be colored. Say, "Not in here," as you point inside the lines. Repeat, "In here? No." "Out here? Yes." You may say this several times to make sure the child understands. After the frame is colored with long thick strokes, paste the picture in the center.

The child may make more pictures, with different colored frames. For example: cut a silhouette of Washington or Lincoln from red construction paper. Color the frame blue. Call attention to the red, white, and blue.

More advanced children may paste a silhouette inside an oval and color outside for the frame; or they may paste fish inside a circle and color the frame.

Balloon Pictures

Materials: paper, crayons

Trace around a tin can or cup with a heavy black crayon. Make four of these circles on a piece of paper. Color a little red in the center of one circle; blue in another; yellow in a third; and green in the fourth. Call the child's attention to the color. Ask him to show you a crayon the same color. Help him if necessary.

Encourage him to color each circle, staying within the lines. When the circles are colored, draw strings, making them balloons. Hang the picture up and use it for color identification. Ask him to show you red or to point to yellow, and so on. Ask, "How many balloons are there? Let's count."

Play a little game. You chant:

> I know a puzzle;
> I know a puzzle;
> I see something red.

The child responds:

> I know your puzzle;
> I know your puzzle;
> It's a balloon that's colored red.

If a child wants to surprise you and point to something else in the room that is red, that's all right. He is thinking. If he can't talk, he may point to something red.

Coloring Embossed Wallpaper

Materials: embossed wallpaper, crayons

Retarded children often get a feeling of pattern by coloring embossed wallpaper. The raised surface, as well as the lines, act as a guide and helps them to get away from "scribble" coloring. When a picture is done well, it may be mounted and displayed. It may also be made into a book cover, place mat, or cover for a scrapbook.

107

PASTING, CUTTING, TEARING, FOLDING PAPER

A retarded child has to learn each skill separately. However, once he has learned two or more skills, he should be given numerous opportunities to combine the skills and to use them in different ways. One handicraft project may require a child to fold a paper, cut or tear it, and then paste parts together. Many jobs done in sheltered workshops require only the skills mentioned in this chapter, especially pasting.

Pasting There are at least two kinds of pasting: (1) covering relatively large areas completely with paste and sticking them onto something else, and (2) pasting small figures in place on a larger object. It is well to use a different method for each type of work.

When a child is going to put paste on a large area, such as a picture to be pasted inside a cardboard playhouse, mix a rather thin solution of wallpaper paste, or mix flour and water paste (see recipe page 109). This paste may be thinned. Cover the work space well with newspapers so that the child can put paste on the very edges of the picture. Give him a 1½-inch paint brush, the kind that is sold in the paint department of a dime store. This type of brush is less expensive than an artist's brush and it holds more paste. Have the child cover the area completely with paste. He may use a sweeping arm motion. When there is enough paste on the paper, have him lift it carefully, place it where it should go, and smooth it, from the center of the picture to the edges, to get out all the bubbles and any excess paste.

When the child is pasting a small object in place, such as putting an eye on a cut-out bunny, put a little library paste on a piece of scrap paper and place it in front of him. Have him apply the paste with his finger, wipe his finger on a rag, put the object in place, paste side down, and then pound it with his clenched fist, saying, "Bang! Bang!" The "bang, bang" gives a climax to his action, which he enjoys. It also helps him to co-ordinate speech and action.

When applying stickers, avoid licking. Apply clean water with either a brush or fingers. After the sticker is in place, complete the action by pounding with the fist and saying, "Bang! Bang!"

Eventually the child may give up saying "bang" as he becomes absorbed in making more intricate objects, such as pasting the sides of an Easter basket together. However, he should have formed the habit of pressing hard on each thing he has pasted to make sure that it will "stay stuck."

PASTE RECIPE. Place ¾ cup of cold water in the top of a double boiler. Add one cup flour. Stir. Gradually add one cup *hot* water. Cook over boiling water for ten minutes, stirring constantly.

If you plan to store pasted objects, add powdered cloves or red pepper to paste. It makes paste offensive to mice.

Medallion

Materials: small paper doily or round piece of brightly colored paper, paste, small picture or seal, ribbon, decorations of confetti, glitter, sequins, or sugar

Have a child paste a small picture in the center of a small paper doily or in the center of a brightly colored paper circle. Punch a hole about ½ inch from the edge of the circle, directly above the center of the picture. Put a piece of ribbon through the hole and tie it in a loop. Let him paste a picture on the other side of the medallion, if he wishes.

To make the medallion more colorful, put a little paste around the edges of the picture, or if paste has "oozed" out around the edges, leave it there. Let the child sprinkle glitter, confetti, sequins, or white or colored sugar around the picture.

Hold the picture over a piece of paper. Shake off the extra decoration. The decoration sticks to the paste and nowhere else. Use the excess decoration for another medallion. This medallion may be used as a Christmas tree decoration.

109

LOCKET. Have a child mount a small medallion with a picture on only one side on cardboard and wear it as a locket.

WALL DECORATION. Have a child make three medallions with pictures on only one side. Do not add the ribbon loop. Space the three mounted pictures on a long piece of ribbon. Paste or staple in place and hang as a picture.

VALENTINE OR GREETING CARD. Have a child paste a medallion, without the ribbon, on construction paper and send it as a valentine or greeting card.

Papier-Mâché Hats

Materials: wallpaper paste; newspaper, and if you wish, thin cotton cloth, wallpaper, construction paper, or used gift wrapping paper; decorations or paint

Mix a thin solution of wallpaper paste. Choose a mold large enough to fit on the head. This may be a medium-sized ball, a pot, or a bowl. Cut four identical circles large enough to fit over the mold, or larger. You can use four circles of newspaper. Or you can use two circles of newspaper for the inside circles; and on the outside use two circles of fairly thin wallpaper, construction paper, gift wrapping paper, or thin cotton cloth. Help the child to do the following where he needs help.

Paste two newspaper circles together, one on top of the other, covering the area completely with paste. These are the inside circles. Put paste on one side of the inside circles. Lay one of the outside circles on the pasted circles. Smooth it. Turn the circles over. Put paste on the other side of the inside circles. Lay the second outside circles on the paste. Smooth it. As the two outside circles have no paste placed directly on them, the project is less messy than any other type of papier-mâché.

Press the four pasted circles over the mold. If you wish, turn up the edges. Or change the style of the hat by changing the position of the circles on the mold. To make a derby, press the circles over a ball. Turn up the edges a little. To make a pill-box, press the circles over a pan. Or create a style of your own by turning part of the brim up, and part down. Or make a hat with a wide brim, or press the circles forward on the mold to make a sunbonnet.

Set the circles aside to dry on the mold for a day or so. Take the hat off the mold and decorate it. You can paint the newspaper hat. Add flowers and ribbons to a lady's hat.

DOLL HATS. Make doll hats the same way, using smaller molds. You can use paper you have decorated (see index) for the outside layers.

NUT CUPS AND BASKETS. Nut cups and small baskets may be made like Papier-Mâché Hats (above). Besides materials listed, you can use paper which you have decorated (see index) for the outside layers. To make a nut cup, choose a small dish or clean empty tin can, such as a tuna can or frozen juice can. For a basket, use a large dish or can, such as a coffee can.

If you would like to add a handle to a basket, punch holes in the sides of the basket when it is dry. Either insert a pipestem—cleaner handle; or cut a construction-paper handle, double thickness, and fasten it in place with round-head paper fasteners.

Cutting Many retarded children find it difficult to cut with scissors. They can make the first snip, but cannot manage to open the scissors and snip again. One way to help them is to give them something that can be cut with one snip.

Cut a strip of heavy construction paper ¾ inch wide. In the beginning, you may have to place the scissors on the thumb and index finger of the child and show him how to open and close them. Hold and guide the paper for him, saying, "open" and "close" repeatedly as he snips. Later he will be able to hold the scissors in his right hand and the paper in his left and snip-snip all by himself.

When he has the idea of snipping, have him cut a pile of little pieces of paper. Use them for Snip-Snip Picture (below), Many-Colored Wastebasket or Plate (page 113), or Molded Papier-Mâché (page 115).

After the child has learned to snip off pieces of paper with one stroke of the scissors, he is ready to learn to cut a strip. Draw parallel lines, about 1 inch apart, on newspaper. Let him cut strips. Later have him cut strips of construction paper. The brightly colored strips may be used for making paper chains, which are just as pretty for room decorations in the spring as they are at Christmas time. The newspaper strips can be used for strip papier-mâché objects (page 117). Although torn strips are better, cut strips may be used.

When the child has learned how to open and close the scissors and cut in a straight line, he is ready to learn how to cut out large and more or less regular outlines.

Snip-Snip Pictures

Materials: large sheet of paper, construction paper, paste, crayons

Draw a picture of a large tree with bare branches. Have the child cut a number of small pieces of yellow, red, and brown paper and paste them along the branches so that the tree looks as if it is all decked out with fall foliage. There might be some leaves on the ground.

CHRISTMAS. Cut a large Christmas tree out of green construction paper. Have the child cut small pieces of brightly colored construction paper and paste them on the tree for decoration and lights. Paste the decorated tree on a piece of larger paper.

VALENTINE'S DAY. Cut out a big red heart. Have the child cut little pieces of white paper and paste them here and there on the heart. Paste the decorated heart on a large sheet of paper. Or make small valentines. Cut a heart the right size to send as a valentine. Have the child cut small pieces of white paper and decorate the heart. Paste the decorated heart in the center of a larger sheet of paper.

Many-Colored Wastebasket

Materials: cardboard carton, paste, shellac, scraps of brightly colored paper—may be colorful ad in magazine or scraps of construction paper

Choose a sturdy carton the right size for a wastebasket. The child cuts a quantity of scraps of brightly colored paper and pastes them onto the box. If there is a play group, several children can help to make one wastebasket. When the carton is covered, shellac it.

OTHER BOXES. Choose the box that is the right size to hold unanswered mail, handkerchiefs, bobby pins, and so forth. The child covers this with scraps of paper as above.

MANY-COLORED PLATE OR SMALL TRAY. *Substitute materials:* three identical paper plates instead of carton or box

The child pastes three identical plates together, one on top of the other. Hold the edges of the plates together with snap clothespins until the paste is dry.

He pastes bits of paper on the top and bottom of the plates, completely covering it. Let the paste dry.

Shellac the plate on the top one day and on the bottom the next. This plate may be used to hold fruit or as a tray for carrying glasses or other small objects. It cannot be washed, but it can be wiped clean with a damp cloth.

Corner-Snip Design

Materials: construction paper or paper hand-decorated, paste

Ask a child to do as you do. Fold a square of paper in half. Fold it in half the other way to make a smaller square. Cut off each corner. A child who has learned to snip a strip of paper into bits should be able to cut off a corner with one snip of the scissors. Open the paper. See how it looks.

Fold the paper again. Snip out a piece of paper along each side. This cutting requires opening and closing the scissors, but it is not as hard as cutting on a line. Open the paper again. See the design!

When you have a design that you like especially well, paste it on construction paper or paper you have decorated (see index). See how the pretty color or colors show through. Use the design for a greeting card or a valentine.

113

Charm Bracelets

Materials: used envelope, crayons or paint

Take a used envelope which has been opened at the end, or reseal one by pasting down the flap. Have the child color or paint the envelope.

Draw lines at 1-inch intervals parallel to the ends of the envelope. Have the child cut along one of the lines. Pick up the piece that is cut off. Open it. See the bracelet! Put it on your arm, or on the child's arm. Encourage her to make more bracelets and wear them when playing house.

Oriental Lantern

Materials: construction paper, paste, two-prong paper fasteners

Fold a piece of construction paper in half the long way. Draw a 1-inch margin at the top of the sheet. Draw vertical lines, at ½-inch intervals, from the fold to this line. Fold the 1-inch margin so that it stands up on each side.

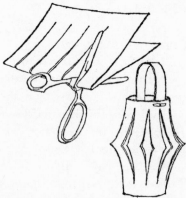

The child starts at the bottom fold and cuts along each vertical line, up to the folded margin line. Learning to cut to a certain line, and no farther, is difficult. After he has cut the paper properly, help him to follow these instructions.

Open the paper. Overlap the two side edges and paste them together. Cut a handle from a double sheet of construction paper. Punch a hole in each end of the handle and holes in the lantern where the handle should be. Attach the handle with two-prong paper fasteners.

BIRD IN CAGE. *Additional materials:* yellow crayon, thread

Cut out the figure of a little bird. Color it yellow on both sides. Punch a hole in the top of its back. Tie a piece of thread through the hole. Suspend the bird from the handle of the lantern so that it is inside a cage. Hang up the bird in the cage. The slightest current of air will make the bird rotate.

BASKET. *Additional material:* oatmeal box

Cut an empty oatmeal box, or any other round box, the height you want the basket to be. Cover it with construction paper or hand-decorated paper (see index). Cut a piece of construction paper or decorated paper ½ inch longer than the distance around the box and 1 inch wider. Make a lantern (page 114). Paste the lantern around the basket. Cut a double handle of construction paper. Fasten in place with two-prong paper fasteners.

Tearing Paper Tearing paper, when torn paper is needed, is good for retarded children. It requires grasping and co-ordination of both hands. It uses many small muscles. It also gives children a chance to destroy something in an acceptable fashion.

The easiest way to use torn paper is for papier-mâché. There are a few other projects where it can also be used.

Molded Papier-Mâché

Materials: newspaper, flour, salt, water, powdered cloves or red pepper

Papier-mâché has a clammy, gooey feeling which most children like. It can be molded like clay and it dries with a hard surface which can be painted.

Tear newspaper into small bits—the smaller the paper, the finer the papier-mâché will be. Soak the torn paper in water, at least overnight. If the paper absorbs all the water, add more.

When you are ready to work with the papier-mâché, pour off the excess water. Rub the paper into a fine pulp. Add some powdered cloves or red pepper to make the flour paste offensive to mice. A drop or two of oil of cloves serves as a preservative for papier-mâché. To three cups of squeezed pulp, add one cup of flour and one third cup salt. Squeeze the paper and salt and flour together until it is well mixed.

115

Roll it around metal knitting needles to make big beads. Or mold snow houses, doll dishes, or fruits and vegetables for a play corner. With imagination you can help a child to make any number of things with this type of papier-mâché.

Hand Puppet

Materials: papier-mâché mixture (page 115), cardboard tube, paint, cloth

You can use any cardboard tube for the base of the puppet. Cut the tube a little longer than a child's finger. Press papier-mâché around the tube in the shape of a head. Leave some at the base of the tube for shoulders to help hold the puppet's costume on. Poke holes in the head for eyes and squeeze the mixture to make a nose. Add bits of mixture for ears.

Set the head away to dry for several days. When it is thoroughly dry, paint it. To make a dress, cut a hole in a square rag and slip it over the puppet's shoulders. Or make a kimona-style costume.

A child may put one or two fingers up into the tube, depending on the size of the tube. His thumb and fingers that stick out form the arms of the puppet.

Willow Tree

Materials: large piece of paper, green paper, paste

Sketch the trunk and branches of a formalized willow tree on a large sheet of paper. The child tears strips of green paper and pastes one end of each strip on a branch of the tree, letting the other end hang down.

Say, "Let's blow on the leaves. See them move!"

Lacy Doily

Materials: paper, paste

Learning to tear on a fold, but not along the fold, requires judgment and self-discipline. Start by tearing newspaper or scrap paper. Later, use colored paper. Encourage child to do as you do.

Take a square piece of paper. Fold it in half. Fold it in half the other way to make a smaller square. Tear out a small piece of paper on a folded edge. Move along the fold. Tear out another piece of paper. Make several small irregular tears along both folds. Be sure to leave part of the paper untorn along each fold. Tear the open edges in a jagged pattern. Open the paper. See the pretty design!

Paste the design on brightly colored construction paper, or hand decorated paper (see index). See the colors show through.

Tear designs in papers with different shapes—a rectangle, a circle, a heart. Paste small designs on construction paper and use them as valentines or greeting cards.

Strip-Papier-Mâché Bowl

Materials: newspaper, wallpaper paste or homemade paste, poster paints, shellac, aluminum foil, water, powered cloves or red pepper

This type of papier-mâché gives a smooth result. Retarded children who have developed a fairly long attention span can achieve excellent results. A bowl or basket made this way may be kept for some time. Work with a child on this, helping him where necessary.

Cut or tear a large number of strips of newspaper about 1 inch wide and of equal length. Use half black and white print and half colored comic paper. Choose a shallow bowl for a mold. Turn the bowl upside down. Soak some of the black and white strips in clear water. Lay them across the bottom

117

of the bowl, extending from one edge to the other, with the edges of strips overlapping, until the mold is covered.

Mix a thin paste adding a little powdered cloves or red pepper to make the paste offensive to mice. Dip some of the colored comic-paper strips into the paste. Let them get gooey. Lay these strips over the first layer of strips, going from edge to edge of the bowl. Overlap the edges of the paper. Smooth each strip as you work. Continue to add layers of pasted strips, alternating black and white strips with comic-paper strips, until you have eight layers.

Set the dish aside for several days to let the paper dry thoroughly. Lift out the bowl. Cut off any extra pieces of paper. Gently sandpaper any rough spots on the surface. Paint the bowl. When the paint is dry, shellac it. You cannot wash this bowl; but you can wipe it with a damp cloth. Line it with aluminum foil and use it to hold crackers, fruit, or any other dry food.

EASTER BASKET. *Additional material:* construction paper, round-headed paper fasteners

Make an Easter basket that should last for years using the above method. You need only five layers of paper. To make a handle, cut a double strip of construction paper. Punch a hole near each end of the handle and holes near the rim of the basket in the places where the handle should be fastened. Attach the handle to the basket with roundheaded paper fasteners.

The handle is for looks! Don't let a child pick up the basket filled with Easter eggs and try to carry it by the handle.

Tunnel

Materials: box, papier-mâché mixture (page 115)

Choose a cardboard box the right size for a tunnel for small toy cars. Cover the workspace with newspaper. Cut out the ends of the box. Set the box upside down on the newspaper. Cover the box completely with papier-mâché mixture. Set the tunnel aside for several days to dry. When it is completely dry, paint it.

You can also use a bowl for a mold. Unlike the box, it will not become a part of the finished product. Cover the bowl only where you want the tunnel to be. You can shape it by cutting the papier-mâché when it is dry.

118

Folding A retarded child who learns how to fold accurately may find this skill very useful later in life. He may learn to iron simple things which require neat folding. He may fold circulars or form letters in a sheltered workshop. A girl may learn to fold material for a hem.

A child must be shown each step of folding. He may watch a parent or teacher and still need help in working by himself. The leader should give verbal instructions along with the demonstration although it may take some time for a child to learn what is meant by "fold in half" or any other direction. A child should also learn to fold on a ruled line. Place a ruler on a line and fold over the ruler.

Wrapping is closely related to folding and, of course, is used frequently. A child should be given a chance to wrap the gifts he makes, wrap articles "bought" in a play-store, and so forth.

Soldier Hat

Materials: newspaper, staples

A retarded child will need to be shown each step in making this hat. However, he will have practice in pressing a fold and will have

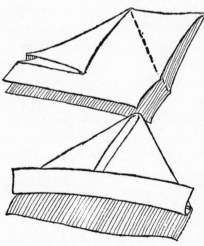

something to wear when he has finished.

Take a double sheet of newspaper, preferably the comic section. Fold it in half, the long way. Place it on a table with the open edges toward you. Mark the center on the fold. Fold the upper left-hand corner down from this center mark. Press the fold with the hands.

Fold the upper right-hand corner down from the center mark. Press the fold. Fold the dangling edges up on each side of the hat to make a brim. Staple this brim in place.

119

WEAVING AND SEWING

Weaving and sewing utilize a common basic skill which requires an understanding of the terms over and under, or up and down, or from the top and from the bottom. If you can develop this understanding and the ability to push a needle up or down as directed, you will give the child the necessary "know how" for these crafts.

Weaving Essentially, all that is required in weaving is moving the thread, yarn, or strip under and over the required number of threads or strips. Begin with a large heavy plastic or leatherette mat with five strips of the same material, but contrasting color. The slits in the mat should be 1½ inches apart and each strip 7½ inches long and 1⅜ inches wide. It is helpful to have two mats. One, which is woven by the leader, serves as a sample which the child tries to reproduce. The retarded child usually learns fairly easily to go over one and under one. If he goes over or under more than one, call his attention to it. "How many did you go over?" When he says, "Two," ask, "How many do we go over?" "One." "Fix it please." The leader should start each strip for the child at this stage.

Most retarded children have difficulty in learning that each time we begin a strip, we do so in an opposite way to the preceding strip. In other words, we start one strip over and the next strip under. Be patient. Call his attention to the preceding strip and ask, "How do we begin this one? Over or under?"

When a child can weave this mat well by himself and without a model, use a smaller square with ½-inch slits. Weave with flat Jack Straws. Then use narrow plastic weaving strips. Next use a paper mat with paper strips. When a child can do all of these things, he is ready to make a pot holder with cotton loops on a frame and to weave with yarn or raffia on a cardboard frame.

Woven Place Mats

Materials: construction paper or wallpaper

Fold a piece of construction paper or wallpaper in half. Cut slits at regular intervals, leaving a margin. Open the paper. Cut strips of another color of paper. Help the child weave the strips into the mat.

Burlap Place Mats

Materials: burlap, yarn, thread

Cut a piece of burlap the desired shape and size for a place mat. Pull out a strand of thread 2 inches from each side.

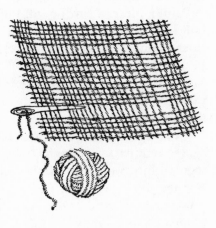

Thread a needle with yarn and have a child weave in and out where you have removed the burlap strands. Machine stitch around the burlap 1 inch from the edges. Have the child fringe the edges of the mat by pulling out the burlap threads as far as the machine stitching.

Sewing Do not urge a child to sew until you are sure that she has developed a fairly long interest span and good eye-hand co-ordination. Many retarded children have faulty vision; take care not to strain eyes.

However, the rewards of sewing are satisfying and lasting. A person can keep something that she has sewn and play with it, wear it, or use it in some other way.

In time, retarded children can learn to make simple household articles and can be helpful with mending. They can learn to sew on buttons. If they can weave, they can learn to darn.

Sewing Cards

Materials: cardboard, yarn

Begin to teach sewing with sewing cards, pieces of heavy paper or cardboard with holes punched in them at regular intervals. Thread a plastic needle, or a large darning needle with yarn. The child puts the needle up through one hole and down the next. Make your own cards in the beginning as the commercial ones are too difficult for beginners.

FRAMED PICTURE. *Additional materials:* paint, picture, paste

Paint a piece of cardboard. Punch holes at regular intervals on all sides about 1 inch from the edge. Paste a picture in the center of the cardboard. Thread a needle with yarn and sew up and down through the holes.

VALENTINE. Cut a heart from heavy red paper. Punch holes at regular intervals around the edge. Sew up and down with white yarn.

GREETING CARDS. Make them like framed picture (above) using heavy paper instead of cardboard.

ORNAMENTS. Cut shapes of diamonds, circles, stockings, trees out of either cardboard or heavy paper. If necessary, paint them. Punch holes around the edges and decorate with yarn sewing. Paste a Christmas seal in the center, or decorate with glitter if you wish.

After a child has learned to do the up-and-down stitch, teach him to do an overcasting stitch, pushing the needle through the holes from the side each time.

Have him make a solid outline by going around the card twice, making the stitch appear on top on one side and on the bottom of the other. Develop cross-stitch with sewing cards.

Greeting-Card Baskets

Materials: used greeting cards, yarn

Hold two heavy greeting cards with the pictures back to back. Trim the cards so that they are the same size. Staple them together in three or four places. Punch holes at regular intervals around the

sides and the bottom. Leave the top open.

Thread a darning needle with yarn, either wool or cotton. Put the yarn through the top hole on one side and tie it securely. Sew the cards together, using an up-and-down stitch or over-and-over stitch. At the last hole, tie a knot in the thread; but do not break it. Fasten it in the first hole, leaving enough slack for a handle on the basket. Remove the staples.

These little baskets may be used in a number of ways at any time of year. They may hold small gifts, or lollipops. Or you can cut out flowers with big stems and tuck them into a basket for a spring greeting. You can hang a basket on a Christmas tree.

OTHER PAPER BASKETS. Make baskets out of heavy construction paper. Or use light-weight cardboard and cover it with construction paper or hand-decorated paper (see index). Make a heart basket for a valentine or a jack-o'-lantern basket with a witch or cat coming out of the top for a Halloween greeting.

WATERPROOF BASKETS. Cut mittens or stockings out of oilcloth or plastic material. Make them into baskets. Put a few evergreen branches in them and hang them outside. Or hang them on a Christmas tree.

Cross-Stitched Towel

Materials: cotton material, embroidery thread, thread

After a child has learned to cross-stitch on a card, let her embroider a towel. If possible, choose cotton material with a check at least ½ inch square. Draw cross-stitches on it. The sewer has the guide of the drawing, plus the color of the material. Use embroidery hoops.

123

Complete each cross-stitch, one at a time. With this method, the sewer can see at once the pattern that she is making.

Instead of hemming the ends, stitch the material on the sewing machine about ½ inch from each end. The child makes fringe by pulling out threads, one by one, as far as the machine stitching.

There are a number of articles that can be embroidered with cross-stitch: luncheon mats, aprons, napkins, small table cloths—to name a few.

Kitty

Materials: old sock, thread, cotton cloth, rubber band, old nylon stockings for stuffiing, paint, or buttons

Take any old sock, one full of holes if you wish, and cut off the top and the foot. Use only the leg portion which should be at least 4 or 5 inches long. The entire kitty is made from this tube. The upper part is its head and the lower part its body. If you don't have an old sock, sew a scrap of cotton cloth into a tube about the size of a sock leg. Help the child do the following.

Turn the tube wrong side out. Sew the top together using an overcast stitch or a running stitch sewing the seam back and forth to make it firm. Turn the sock right side out. To make ears, sew across the corners at the top, pulling the thread a little. Fasten the thread.

Making the face may require help. Paint the features with latex or fabric paints. Or sew on button or cloth eyes. Embroider a nose. Sew long loops with double thread under the nose for whiskers. Cut the loops and tie the threads near the nose so that they won't come out.

Stuff the kitty loosely. A kitty with nylon stuffing can be washed and will dry quickly. Slip a rubber band over kitty's head and down to the point where his neck should be. If necessary, double the rubber band in order to pull the sock in a little. Cut a strip of cotton cloth with pinking shears. Tie this strip of cloth over the rubber band and in a big bow. Sew a strip of cloth on kitty for a tail. Or braid strips of cloth and sew the braid in place for a tail.

Running-Stitch Embroidery

Materials: pre-hemmed towel or place mat, embroidery thread

Machine stitch a towel or place mat. Draw a row of stitches of irregular lengths across the ends or around the edges. Put the material in an embroidery hoop.

Thread a needle with two strands of embroidery thread, doubled so that it won't come out of the needle. The sewer uses the same method as she did on the sewing card, except that now she has lines, not holes to guide her.

Draw a second line of stitches when the first row is completed. Use a harmonizing, but different color of embroidery floss for the second row of stitches. Make either three or five row of stitches to complete the embroidery on the towel or place mat.

CLAY CRAFT

Clay is a material that can be used with a group of retarded children who represent a wide range of ability. All are working with clay, but with various degrees of skill. Working with clay is a satisfying solitary activity for a child who has been given preliminary help. Almost every child gets pleasure in discovering that clay will respond to touch and that he can make it do what he wants it to do. It offers a wide scope for imagination and serves a valuable function as a manipulative hand and finger exercise. Clay work also helps a child to learn the meaning of such words as push, pull, squeeze, pinch, roll, and so forth.

Retarded children need a great deal of preliminary experience with plasticine (page 85) or other commerical clays that are fairly malleable and can be used over and over again. When a child has learned to use these clays, he can work with self-hardening clay which is permanent. There are many varieties available at craft and

125

school-supply houses. The Mexican kind is smooth and a pretty red; many others are fibrous. Or you can mix your own.

RECIPE. Mix thoroughly one-fourth pound of dextrine (a kind of sugar available at drugstores) into five pounds of dry clay powder (available at craft stores). Add one and three-fourths pints of water.

This mixture must be used fairly soon after mixing as it goes sour after a week or so and develops an unpleasant ordor.

PAINTING. Clay objects may be painted with poster paint or latex paint. You can get unusual effect with sponge painting (page 99), and by making different kinds of strokes with the brush (page 105). If a dish is to hold water, it must receive several coats of shellac and then be heavily waxed.

ANTIQUE FINISH. To get a mottled, antique finish, mix some powered poster paint with paste wax. Rub it on the dish until you have a pleasing effect. Follow with coats of clear wax until you have a dull luster.

Easy Self-hardening Clay Projects
Materials: clay, paint

A child can make many objects that are no harder than the things he made of plasticine. It can also be used instead of plaster of Paris as the base for an eggshell favor or candle holder (pages 142, 143).

BEADS. Roll clay beads. Push a narrow dowel through them and remove the dowel. Let clay harden. Paint.

PAPER WEIGHT. Roll clay into the shape of a snow man or an angel. Give the angel aluminum foil wings and a halo made of a small drapery ring.

Pinch Bowl
Materials: self-hardening clay, paint, shellac

Hold a ball of self-hardening clay in one hand. Stick the thumb of the other hand into the center of the ball. Press with your thumb on the inside of the clay and with your fingers on the outside. Rotate the ball, forming it into a bowl. Avoid pressing the clay wall too thin. If it does get too thin, squeeze the clay together and start again.

When you have a bowl with a pleasing shape, stop. Put the clay on a clay board to dry. If a child is still interested in working with clay, give him another ball for further experimenting and practice.

Paint the bowl. If you want it to hold water, give it several coats of shellac.

Oblong Dish

Materials: self-hardening clay, paint

Assemble the equipment before you start to work. Take two pieces

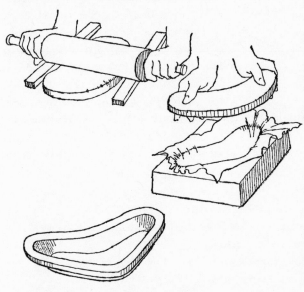

of lath about 12 inches long and ¼ inch thick. Place them about 8 inches apart on a clay board. The end of an apple crate makes an excellent clay board.

Make a paper pattern, not larger than 6 inches wide and 10 inches long, for the bottom of the dish. I r r e g u l a r shapes are pleasing. Trace it on the lid of a shoe box. Cut it out, being careful not to damage the lid of the box or break the sides. The cut-out portion of the lid is the pattern for the dish. The remaining portion of the lid is the mold.

Set the mold right side up. Lay a piece of wet cheesecloth over the mold. Help the child do the following.

Place a lump of clay on the clay board between the pieces of lath. Roll the clay with a rolling pin or other roller. The lath acts as tracks and makes it impossible to roll the clay thinner than the thickness of the lath. The clay, therefore, has uniform thickness. Place the cardboard pattern on the rolled clay. Allowing at least a 1-inch margin, cut around the pattern. Remove the outside clay. Remove the pattern.

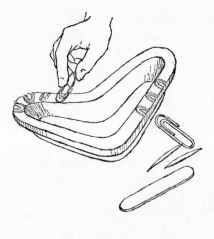

Pick up the remaining clay and place it on the cheesecloth over the hole in the mold. The center of the clay will sag down to the workspace. The lip, or outside edges of the dish lie flat on the mold. Press the clay gently to make sure that the bottom is resting flat on the table. The dish will be as deep as the lid is high.

There are many ways to make decorative indentions on the lip. Press the clay around the edges with a paper clip, or the edge of a tongue depressor, or the eraser end of a pencil, and so forth. Set the dish aside to dry. When the clay is well set, but not thoroughly dry, remove the dish from the mold and take off the cheesecloth. Let the clay dry thoroughly. Sand rough spots. Paint or decorate the dish (page 126).

Leaf Dish

Materials: self-hardening clay, paint

Roll out self-hardening clay as described in oblong dish (page 127).

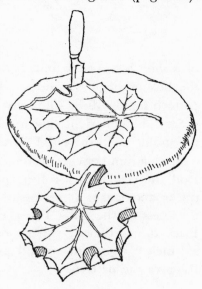

Gently press a large leaf, veined side down, into the clay. Cut around the leaf with a knife or blunt scissors, making the stem wider and longer than it would naturally be. Remove the excess clay. Gently lift off the leaf. Curl the stem over to make a handle. Lift the edges of the leaf slightly and support with sticks until the clay is dry. Sand any rough spots gently, being careful not to injure the pattern of the veins.

Paint the dish or rub color into it (page 126). See how the veins have a darker tone than the rest of the dish.

128

HAMMERING AND SANDING

Hammering and sanding are acceptable noisy and vigorous activities which provide excellent release from tension and help to develop both large and small muscles. However, they are tiring and a child should not be encouraged to work on a project too long on a single day.

Roofing nails, short thick nails with flat heads, are best for beginning hammering projects. At first, a parent or teacher may start the nail by pounding the tip into the wood. The child drives it into the wood. A child, learning to pound, holds the nail in one hand in the position to pound it into the wood. He holds the hammer in the other hand, near the head; and then taps, taps the nail lightly until it stands by itself. He then holds the hammer farther down the handle and drives the nail into the wood.

Sanding offers an opportunity to teach concepts of rough and smooth. Before sanding a piece of wood, rub your hand over it and have the child do the same. Talk about the fact that the wood is rough and that you are going to make it smooth. Check frequently as you work to see if the wood is at last getting smooth.

Start by sanding a flat piece of wood. The end of an apple crate is excellent. Talk about how you are going to use it—for a board on which to roll out clay for modeling, a peg board, or a bread board. Teach the child to sand by wrapping sandpaper around a block of wood. Also let him sand by holding the sandpaper in his hand.

If you finish an article with shellac or sealer, have the child wax it well when it is dry—more rubbing exercise.

Street Number or Name Sign

Materials: ¾ inch lumber; lumber 2 inches thick, 2 inches wide, and 18 inches long; glue; two large nails; roofing nails; shellac or sealer

The street number or name of a family is printed with roofing nails on this sign which can be stuck into the family lawn. Use two pieces of pre-cut lumber—a piece of ¾ inch lumber the desired size for the sign, and a post made from lumber 2 inches wide and 2 inches thick. Saw the post into an 18-inch length. Measure 5 inches from the bottom of the post. Draw a line around the post. Work the post into a point with a saw and file. Sand both pieces of wood.

Draw the numbers and letters on the wood. If you think it is necessary, draw a dot where each nail head should be placed. Pound roofing nails into the wood along the lines. Shellac the sign or finish it with sealer.

BOOK ENDS. Make book ends from thick pieces of wood. Decorate with roofing-nail initials.

Boats

Materials: wood, nails, glue, paint, string, spools

A variety of boats can be made from scrap lumber. A small piece of wood with a nail pounded into one end becomes a barge which a child can pull in the water. To make a railing, pound a row of nails around the edge and wind a string from nail to nail. See if the barge will float. If it sinks, unwind the string and pull out some of the nails.

To make a steamboat, choose three pieces of wood that can be piled on top of each other; a small piece of wood, a piece of wood a little larger than the first, and a third piece of wood larger than the second. Glue the decks together. Then nail together with long thin nails. Glue on empty spools for smokestacks.

A child can paint the boats, or play with them as they are.

Apple-crate Shelves

Materials: apple crate; paint, shellac, or sealer

Sand an apple crate. Either paint it with latex paint, shellac it, or apply sealer. Use it to hold toys.

Cheese-Box Gifts Grocers receive creamed cheese in small sturdy wooden boxes which may be used for many articles. A child can sand off the printing if he works hard.

PLANT HOLDER. *Materials:* cheese box, paint, aluminum foil

Sand a cheese box. Paint it, or shellac it, or apply sealer. When it is dry, line it with aluminum foil. Fill with earth and add plants.

COLLECTION WHAT-NOT. *Materials:* three cheese boxes, glue, paint

Make a what-not to hold a collection of small objects—such as rocks or shells—out of three cheese boxes piled one on top of the other. Sand the portions of the cheese boxes which will form the outside of the what-not. Glue the unsanded portions of the boxes together. Hold in place with clamps or weight them down until the glue is dry. Paint or shellac the what-not or apply sealer.

KNIFE-AND-FORK HOLDER. *Materials:* two cheese boxes, glue, paint

Make a knife-and-fork holder out of two cheese boxes glued side by side. Sand the portions of the boxes which will form the outside of the holder. Glue the unsanded portions together. Hold them together with clamps or weight them down until the glue is dry. Paint or shellac the holder or apply sealer.

131

VI. Handicraft for Special Reasons

AFTER A CHILD HAS LEARNED THE VARIOUS HANDICRAFT SKILLS, THE emphasis is no longer placed on how to do things. The child cuts, pastes, or paints because he wants to make something—a design or a picture, a holiday favor or toy, or something else. Or he follows directions because he wants to see what happens when he lets colors run together or what happens when he folds paper and cuts it a certain way.

Of course there should be no sharp difference, from a child's point of view, between learning handicraft skills and making things for a purpose. A parent or teacher never says, "Now we shall practice cutting." From the start, a leader should try to make some use of everything that a child creates, stress that the colors are pretty, or in some way make the project seem purposeful when it is completed.

However, the child's point of view does change, without his knowing it, as he gains self-confidence in handling equipment. When he no longer worries about how he should hold scissors, he can concentrate on what he is cutting and why he is cutting it. When he has reached this stage, he makes rapid growth in the social and mental areas mentioned in the introduction of Learning Handicraft Skills.

SURPRISE!

Retarded children love a surprise, especially if you, an adult, are still capable of enjoying the wonderment of colors that flow together in unexpected combinations, designs that look different double, and materials which combine in different ways. The following projects all have a "Let's do this and see what happens" approach. They give a child a chance to create, often accidentally; because each time that he does a project, the results are different.

Encourage a child to note and talk about the difference between two projects which were made by the same method. Encourage him to see likenesses, differences, and relationships in a single project. Encourage him to talk about these relationships. "What is the prettiest color?" "What does this shape look like?" Help him to use his imagination.

Although the emphasis in this chapter is on surprise and creating, try to use the work which the child does in as many ways as possible: as decorative paper, a background for a pasted picture, or, in some cases, a display on a bulletin board.

Stained-Glass Windows

Materials: white paper, water, water colors, black construction paper, paste

Using a wide paint brush, completely cover a sheet of white paper with clear water. Put daubs of different colors of water colors here and there on the sheet. Use clean primary colors—red, blue, yellow. Crumple the paper. Now, open it.

See how the colors have run together, making different designs with many shades of each color. Let the paper dry.

To make a stained-glass window, cut a simple design for a church window out of black construction paper. Paste it onto the painted paper. Trim the painted paper to match the black paper. If it is Easter or Christmas time, cut out a religious picture and mount it on construction paper. Make two stained-glass windows. Hang the picture on the bulletin board. Hang a stained-glass window on either side.

You can use the painted paper in other ways: as gift-wrapping paper, a place mat, a background on which to paste a silhouette, the outside paper for a hat or nut cup (page 110), or for any other project calling for decorative paper.

Ink Blot or Paint Design

Materials: paper, ink, or paint

Fold a piece of paper in half. Open it and put a drop of ink or paint on one side. Refold the paper. Rub it. Open the paper. See the design! What does it look like?

Transfer Design

Materials: paper; soft pencil, colored chalk, or crayon

Fold a piece of paper in half. Open it and draw half of a picture or design on one side, near the fold, using a soft pencil, heavy wax crayon, or chalk. Refold the paper with the drawing inside. Lay the folded paper on a hard flat surface such as a table or desk. Rub the paper hard several times with the side of a pencil or rhythm stick. Open the paper. The design is repeated on the other side. Trace the duplicated half so that both sides of the design are of equal darkness.

Color inside the lines you have drawn; or go over the outline with heavy wax crayon and paint within the lines. Or cut out the design and paste it onto a sheet of construction paper. Make it into a greeting card. Make a heart and use it on a valentine; or a tree or bell and use it on a Christmas card.

Figure Appear

Materials: paper, pencil, or crayon

Put a cardboard figure in a used envelope or fold a sheet of paper and put the figure between the two halves. Hold the cardboard in place with one hand. Rub over the figure with a crayon held in the other hand. See the figure appear!

Next try putting a leaf between the sheets of paper or in a used envelope. It will be harder to hold the leaf in place than it was the cardboard figure; but it will be fun to see all the veins appear.

Try rubbing a penny placed between the halves of folded paper or in an envelope. Use a soft pencil. It is hard to hold the penny because it is small; but it is fun to "make money"—even play money.

Lighted Christmas Tree

Materials: green construction paper, red, blue, and yellow tissue paper, paste, thread, stars, glitter, or other decorations

Cut a Christmas tree out of green construction paper. Punch holes in it here and there, one for each light on the tree. Tear or cut small swatches of different colored tissue paper. Paste the pieces over the holes on one side of the tree. These will look like many colored lights.

Turn the paper over. Decorate the tree by pasting stars or other shapes where there are no "lights." Or put paste where there are no "lights" and sprinkle on glitter or other decorations.

Punch a hole in the center top of the tree. Tie a thread through the hole. Hang the tree in a sunny window. See the sunlight shine through the tissue paper making it look like little lights on the tree!

VARIATION. If you wish to hang the tree where it will show clearly from the outside as well as inside a room, cut a tissue-paper tree the same size and shape as the construction-paper tree and paste it over the punched holes. The child may not be able to cut the thin paper, but he can learn that different papers have different weights. The "lights" on the tree will be the same color. But the backside of the tree will be neater than one covered with swatches of different colored tissue paper.

135

String Designs

Materials: paper, colored chalk, or unwrapped crayon

Wrap a string around a breadboard, first one way and then the other, and crisscross. Or wrap it around a cardboard shirt board or other piece of cardboard. Lay a piece of paper over the string and thumb tack it onto the board; or hold the paper in place on the cardboard with paper clips.

With a piece of colored chalk, or with the long side of a piece of unwrapped crayon, rub back and forth over the string until the paper is covered. See the design appear!

There are other ways to make string designs. Fold a sheet of paper. Open it. Drop string in a design on one half of the paper. Refold the paper. Rub as before.

Or drop a piece of string onto a table or board. Lay circles or other forms cut from construction paper near the string. Cover the string and paper figures with a pieces of paper. Rub the paper with chalk or crayon as above. See the design, now. Repeat the project, shifting the paper after part of it has been covered. See what a difference the change of position makes in the design.

Scrape-away Picture

Materials: paper, crayons, poster paint, soap powder

Prepare a mixture of soap powder and paint, about one half cup of poster paint and one tablespoon of soap powder. (Detergents do not work well.) Cover a sheet of paper completely with many colors of wax crayons. Paint over the crayoning with the above preparation of soap and paint. Without the soap, the paint will not stick to the wax. Let the paint dry.

When the paint is dry, thumbtack a stencil to the painted paper. Scrape out the picture or design within the stencil by rubbing the paint away with the side of a paper clip or with blunt scissors. A many-colored picture appears.

Or thumbtack a solid form on the paper. Scrape away the surrounding area. A many-colored background appears.

Crayon and Paint Picture

Materials: paper, crayons, water colors

Draw a picture with wax crayons, but do not color the background of sky, grass, or sea. Color every part of each figure heavily. When the coloring is finished, paint the background with water colors, brushing straight across the paper. The paint will not stick to the crayon.

Make a black and white design, or the picture of trees and bushes covered with snow on a winter night. Make the forms with white crayon. Brush over the crayoning with black or dark blue water colors or poster paints. See the white appear?

You can use these designs as decorated paper for wrapping gifts or for making many projects. You can use them for the background for a cut-out picture.

Cut Designs

Materials: paper, crayon, paste

Fold a piece of paper in half. Using heavy black crayon, draw an outline of half of a simple figure, for example—half a triangle, with

the center on the fold. Ask the child to cut on the line, not the fold. If he is just learning to cut, ask him to show you where he will cut. Have him trace the line with his finger. Ask him, "What is it going to be when we open it? Can you guess?"

When the figure has been cut out, open the paper. See how the figure looks when it is double. Draw and then have him cut out another figure—half a diamond, then a square, an oval or egg, or a circle or ball.

You can advance to harder forms, drawing half a heart, a tulip, a flower with jagged petals, or a Christmas tree. If a design or picture is pretty, or well-cut, help the

137

child to mount it on construction paper. Draw a string on a circle to make it into a balloon, or a stick to make a lollipop. Draw a tail on a diamond to make a kite. Add leaves and a stem to a flower. Use flowers for greeting cards, hearts for valentines, and trees for Christmas cards.

Rainbow Transfer

Materials: paper, crayons

Color a sheet of paper with stripes of bright colors. Be sure that the crayoning is heavy and solid. Place the colored paper, color side down, on another sheet of paper. Using a sharp pencil, draw lines on the clean side of the paper. Bear down hard. You can make a picture, or just makes lines. Be sure that at least some of them go across the stripes. When you have drawn all that you wish, lift the paper. See the new picture in many colors.

If a child has trouble with the paper slipping, either clip the papers together with paper clips or thumbtack them to a board.

Folded-Paper String Painting

Materials: poster paint, paper

Fold a piece of paper in half. Open it. A child dips a piece of string about 15 inches long into a pan of paint. He then holds the string at full length and lowers it onto one side of the paper in a kind of S motion, leaving one end of the string hanging out from the bottom of the paper. Refold the paper.

The leader holds his hand on top of the paper and asks the child to put one hand on top of his and press down hard. The child grabs the string with his other hand and pulls it out. Open the paper. See what happened.

When the paint dries, dip another string into a different but harmonizing color of paint. Repeat the above. The results of this type of painting often look like lilies or Japanese art. Different effects may be gained by using a second color before the first is dry and by using more than two colors.

HOLIDAYS AND CHANGING SEASONS

Retarded children, as a rule, do not grasp a concept of months. However, they do develop a "calendar" sense. They gradually come to realize that one season follows another, and that each season brings with it changes in the appearance of the outdoors, in the weather, and in what they themselves wear and do. They also know that during certain seasons there are special days for which people prepare. Brothers and sisters, if there are any, make holiday decorations and holiday favors which they bring home from school, troop meetings, and so forth. The retarded child at home or at school also wants to make decorations and favors, and he should have the opportunity to do so.

Because a retarded child may not grasp the full concept of the meaning of a holiday, choose the aspect which he understands and which appeals to him. For example, Thanksgiving usually means a big dinner to a retarded child. Therefore, center handicraft or art work around fruits and other food for which we are thankful, rather than around Pilgrims and Indians.

Encouraging retarded children to get ready for holidays and to make things that remind them of different seasons helps them to become aware of the passing of time and also to note the changes that are taking place in the world outside and in the stores, school, and home. Helping to get ready for holidays is one way that retarded children can truly enter into and contribute to family fun.

Each family has its own special-day calendar, which may include many days not mentioned in this section. Few families make favors for Fourth of July, but your family can. You can make cards and favors for religious days celebrated in your own family circle. Or you can develop your own special days. Aunt Jane may always consider her visit a "special day" because of the surprise favor she found at her place at dinner time.

Heart on Heart Valentine

Materials: three different colors of construction paper, paste, glitter, or other decorations, flower seal

Cut out three hearts, each a different color, of identical shapes but different sizes. To do this, make a scrap-paper pattern. Trace around it on construction paper. Trim ½ inch or 1 inch from the edge of the pattern heart. Trace around this pattern on construction paper. Again trim ½ inch or 1 inch from the edge of the pattern heart and trace around this on construction paper. Cut out the construction paper hearts.

Paste the middle-sized heart in the center of the largest one. Paste the smallest heart in the center of the middle-sized one. Paste a flower seal or other small picture in the center of the smallest heart.

Sprinkle a little glitter on the valentine. If any of the paste slipped out from under the edges while you were trying to center a heart, the glitter will stick to the paste. Shake the valentine over a clean sheet of paper. Extra glitter will fall off. Save it.

Of course, valentines do not have to be hearts. They may be circles, squares or any shape. A retarded child cannot be expected to trim the edges to make the pattern. He may be able to trace around a pattern and cut out a heart. You may want to make this just a pasting exercise—plus training in which is larger and smaller.

Make-Believe Kite
Materials: construction paper, rag, string

Cut a kite from construction paper. Color the cross sections on either side of the paper. Punch a hole in the top and tail of the kite.

Tear a rag into a long strip. Tie one end onto the tail of the kite. Tie a string about a yard long into the top of the kite. As the child runs with the kite, the tail flies out behind.

Flying Bird
Materials: paper, crayons, yard long string, small stick

Fold a piece of paper in half. Draw the picture of a bird with the bottom of the breast on the fold. Draw large wings. Draw a dotted line at the base of the wings. Have the child cut out the bird, being careful not to cut along the fold. Then help him follow these directions:

Set the cutout on the table in front of you. Fold the wing nearest to you down. It may help you to place a ruler on the dotted line and fold over the ruler. Turn the bird over. Fold the other wing toward you. Lay one end of the string between the halves so that it extends past the beak. Paste the two halves of the body of the bird together so that the string is pasted between them. Do not put any paste on the wings.

140

Draw a great big eye on the bird. Color the rest of his head. Turn him over. Draw an eye on this side. Color the rest of his head. Now color his body and wings on both sides.

Tie the loose end of the string to the end of a small stick. Spread the bird's wings. The child holds the stick at its free end and runs, letting the bird fly after him.

Bunny Face

Materials: pre-cut bunny ears, construction paper or hand-decorated paper, facial tissues, paste, two matching buttons, scraps of construction paper, glue

141

Put a fairly thin mixture of wall-paper paste or other runny paste in a small dish. Draw a circle on colored construction paper or hand-decorated paper. A child can trace around a dish or any other round thing.

Now, make bunny fur. Tear pieces of facial tissue into bits. Pick up a small bunch of tissue with the tips of your fingers. Dip the part of the paper which you are not holding into the paste. Press the facial tissue onto the paper, *inside* the circle. Fill the circle with other small bunches of torn facial tissue. Put your fingers around the outside of the circle and press the tissue into a round ball.

Paste the pre-cut bunny ears in place. Cut a little nose from a scrap of construction paper. Paste it in place. Cut six narrow strips of construction paper for whiskers. Put paste on the tip of each strip. Paste the tips under the nose. Put glue onto identical buttons —pink or blue if you have them. Press them down into the "fur" for eyes, or cut out construction paper eyes and paste in place.

Eggshell Favors

Materials: plaster of Paris, water, eggshells, dye, paint

Eggshell favors may hold miniature bouquets; they may be used as little nut cups; or they may be filled with jelly beans or other small candies at Easter time. It is easy to make one for each member of the family at home. If they are made in school, each child should be given a small box so that he can carry it home without breaking it.

When you are cooking, crack the eggs so that one part is bigger than the other. Save the larger halves, and dye them as you would Easter eggs.

Mix a small amount of plaster of Paris, following the directions on the package. Be sure to stir the plaster into the water and not

142

the water into the plaster. Add a drop or two of poster paint to the water to color the plaster. Drop a small mound of plaster of Paris onto the top of a tin can, wax paper, or some other material to which the plaster will not stick. Place a dyed eggshell in the plaster in a tilted position. Continue until you have all the eggshells placed in plaster. You may need to gently press the eggshells into the soft plaster to make them stand in the position you wish. Let the plaster dry. These dainty favors will add color to a dining table. Or you could place them elsewhere for spring decorations. You can use self-hardening clay (page 126) instead of plaster of Paris.

CANDLE DECORATION. *Additional materials:* pine cones, candle

For a Christmas favor, place pine cones around a little mound of plaster of Paris. Place a candle in the center of the mound. Hold it straight up until it will stand alone in the plaster.

May Baskets

Materials: waxed-paper cup, clean cottage-cheese container or small, clean tin can; round doily, circle of pretty paper or colored baking cup; aluminum foil or crepe paper; cellophane tape; thin wire or pipe stem cleaner

May baskets are fun to make and fun to deliver in the old-fashioned way. On the first of May, a child fills a May basket with flowers, goes to the home of a friend, rings the door bell, sets the basket near the door, then watches for the friend to come to the door and wonder who on earth left the flowers. If the flowers are in a water repellent basket, they will stay fresh for some time.

143

You can use a waxed-paper cup, a clean cottage-cheese carton, or a small clean tin can—such as frozen juices come in. Punch holes in the side of the container, near the rim, and insert a thin wire or pipe stem cleaner for a handle.

Choose a doily or circle of pretty paper that is bigger than the top of the container. Or if you are using a small cup or tin can, use a paper baking cup. Set the container in the center of the circle and draw around it. Cut from the center of this circle to the line you drew, dividing the circle into eight pie-shaped sections. Slip the circle onto the can with the points of the circle pointing toward the bottom. Fasten circle near the rim of the container with cellophane tape. You may want to prepare this much ahead of time.

Wrap the sides of the container with aluminum foil or crepe paper, allowing the bottom edge to come under the can. Foil will stay in place by itself. Hold paper in place with cellophane tape. Cut a strip of paper and tie a bow under the circle. Twist a strip of paper or foil around the handle. Put some water in the basket and fill it with flowers.

Flower-Greeting Card

Materials: thin construction paper, paste

Cut four strips of construction paper, 4 inches long and 1/2 inch wide. Round the edges. These are petals for a large flower. To curl the petals, place a ruler on its edge near the center of a petal. Hold the ruler with the left hand. Pull the paper from under the ruler with the right hand. The end of the paper will curl. Curl the other end the same way. Curl the ends of the remaining strips.

Paste the center of one strip on the center of another strip so that the strips are at right angles. Paste the centers of the remaining strips across these strips to form a flower with curled petals. Cut a small construction-paper circle and paste it in the center of the flower. Or cut a very narrow strip of paper. Put a little paste in the center of the flower. Snip off small pieces of the strip, letting them land in the paste.

Cut a piece of construction paper larger than the flower. Paste the flower on the paper. Write a Mother's Day, get-well, or Easter greeting on the card.

144

WIGS AND WINGS. You can use this method of curling paper whenever you want curled paper—for hair on masks, wigs for small dolls, or wings for angels or dragon flies.

Face Mask

Materials: newspaper, pink or white paper toweling, Saran Wrap or wax paper, poster paint, paste, elastic

This funny face mask will fit the person for whom it is intended because it is made especially for him. Cover the work space with newspaper or oil cloth.

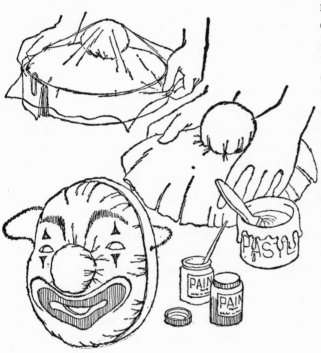

Fold a sheet of newspaper into eighths, lengthwise. Hold this strip under the child's chin and around his face. Overlap the ends and hold them in place with big paper clips. This is the outer mold for the mask. Lay it on the work space. Help him do the following where he needs help.

Fill the center with crumpled newspapers. Wad a piece of paper for a nose. Set it on the face about a fourth of the distance between the forehead and the chin. Tear strips of newspaper. Paste them over the wad to hold the nose in place.

Cover the mold, including the oval ring you wrapped around the head, completely with Saran Wrap. (Wax paper will do but it does not shape up as easily as Saran Wrap.) Crumple it around the nose as best you can and tuck the edges under the oval ring, keeping the shape of the face for the mask.

Cut three oval pieces of newspaper large enough to cover the face and come down over the oval ring. Make them extra large to make sure that they will cover the nose. Cut an identical shape from white or pink paper toweling. It is all right to use two pieces. (You can use four newspaper-ovals, but paper toweling gives a better painting surface than newspaper.) Paste these four ovals together, applying thin paste with a paint brush. Lift the four circles and lay them on the mold with the oval made of toweling on top. Press them down over the mold, smoothing the folds around the nose and around the edges. If the folds tend to come undone, hold them in place by sticking straight pins into the mold. The mask will have deep wrinkles, but it is supposed to be a funny face. Set the mask aside to dry.

When the mask is thoroughly dry, remove the pins and then remove the mold which was covered by Saran Wrap. Trim the edges of paper which extended beyond the mold. Cut a strip of newspaper or toweling about 3 inches wide and long enough to go around the mask. Cover this well with thin paste. Paste it around the edge with about 1½ inches pasted on the outside and the other half folded over and pasted on the inside of the mask. This strip gives the mask a finished edge which helps to hold the folds in place. Let the mask dry again.

Cut out the eyes and mouth. Paint the face with poster paints. Punch holes in the side of the mask, near the ears, and insert an elastic strip. Put the mask on the child's head and adjust the elastic.

A person may wear a mask for Halloween, or at any other time of year when he is playing "Make believe." You can also use a mask for a decoration. Fill a vase with corn stalks and weeds. Stand the face in front of the vase. It will look as if the funny face has acquired a wig.

Bowl of Fruit for Thanksgiving

Materials: different colored construction paper, paste

Draw pictures of fruit on different colored construction paper. Draw a big bowl or basket.

The child cuts out the bowl and pastes it on a full sheet of construction paper. He cuts out the various fruits and pastes them in place on the picture. If his span of interest is short, he can cut and paste one picture a day.

VARIATION. Cut pictures of fruit out of white paper. The child colors or paints the fruit and then pastes each piece in place.

Hanging Greens

Materials: small frozen orange juice can; aluminum foil or water-proof paint; evergreen branches, longest about 6 inches; one yard ribbon

Remove the top and bottom of the can, making sure that the edges are smooth. Cut a few evergreen branches with the longest being about 6 inches. Cut a yard of ribbon.

Cover the can with aluminum foil, or paint it with water-proof paint. Put the ribbon through the can and tie it in a loop with a bow on top. The decoration will hang with the bow on top and the can in a horizontal position.

Insert the ends of the greens into the can from both ends so that the greens spread out into a bushy decoration. If you wish, add small ornaments, artificial berries, or any other water-proof decoration. Hang the greens outside the door. Remember the back or side door can be decorated as well as the front. Or hang them inside over a mirror, as a picture or from the lock on a window. You can also make fall decorations with small branches of colored leaves.

Center Piece

Materials: long, flat potato, cardboard, aluminum foil, greens, other decorations

Choose a long, flat potato for the base of a center piece. Cut a

147

piece of cardboard a little larger than the potato. Cover it with aluminum foil.

Trim small branches of evergreens to the length that you want the center piece to be. Stick them into the potato so that they will make a bushy arrangement. Place the potato on the cardboard that is covered with aluminum foil. Add colorful decorations if you wish—artificial flowers or silver leaves. Or stick fresh cranberries on pins. Push them into the decoration where they will look best.

OTHER BRANCHES. You can arrange branches of colored fall leaves the same way. Do not try to make a large arrangement.

Soda-Straw Chain

Materials: paper drinking straws, different colored construction paper, yarn

A combination of soda straws and colored geometrical figures, strung on yarn, makes a colorful chain for a Christmas tree. Use pre-cut straws and figures. Draw a number of circles or stars, 1½ inches across, on a piece of construction paper. Use only one type of figure. Make a pile of four or six pieces of different colors of construction paper, placing the paper with the drawing on top. Cut out the figures, four or six at a time. Put a paper clip on each group as you cut. The colors will remain in identical order as the child works. Punch a hole with a paper punch in the center of the figures. Cut soda straws into 1-inch lengths.

Thread a piece of yarn on a bobby pin. Pull it double. Put a straw on the yarn. Tie it near the end of the yarn, leaving enough yarn to make a loop.

The child adds a paper figure, then a straw to the chain until the yarn is covered except for the loop at each end. The colors will appear in consecutive order if each pile of paper is kept in order. Remove the bobby pin.

The chain may dangle straight down from a branch of a tree. Or it may be draped from branch to branch, held in place by the loops at the ends.

Shiny Ornaments

Materials: aluminum foil, lightweight cardboard, string, ribbon, glue, decorations

Draw small Christmas wreaths or other figures on lightweight cardboard, such as shirt boards or cereal boxes. Cut them out. Cut two aluminum-foil figures a little larger than the cardboard ones.

Have the child lay the cardboard cutout on the aluminum foil cutout. Wherever there is a curve, cut the foil from the edge to the cardboard. Have the child wrap the edges of the foil over the cardboard and press it down. Cover the other side of the cardboard the same way. The foil will be crinkly.

Punch a hole in the top center of the figure. Put a string through the hole and tie it in a loop. Tie a ribbon on the wreath if you wish or glue on any other decorations.

GIFTS AND PLAYTHINGS

Pencil Holder

Materials: clean, empty tin can (soup can or small-sized spaghetti can) ; wallpaper, gift wrapping, or hand-decorated paper; paste; glue; felt, or other thick cloth; shellac

Choose an empty, clean tin can the right size for a pencil holder. A soup can or small-sized spaghetti can is best; but you can use a can a little larger, or a little smaller.

Cut a piece of pretty paper 1 inch longer than the can is high and wide enough to wrap around the can and overlap 1 inch. You can use wallpaper, discarded gift-wrapping paper, or hand-decorated paper (see index). Finger painting done in shades of brown looks something like leather.

Put paste on the wrong side of the paper. Wrap the paper around the can, overlapping the outer edge. Be sure that the bottom of the paper comes exactly to the bottom of the can. Fold the paper which extends over the top of the can down into the can.

Cut a piece of felt or other heavy cloth the size of the bottom of the can. Glue this onto the can. The cloth prevents the can's scratching the desk on which the holder will be placed.

If you shellac the paper, it will last longer.

Shopping Bag

Materials: large, heavy-paper bag, heavy twine, paper, paste, crayons

Decorated shopping bags may be made and given as gifts any time of the year. Or a child can use them to carry home the things which he has made in school or at camp.

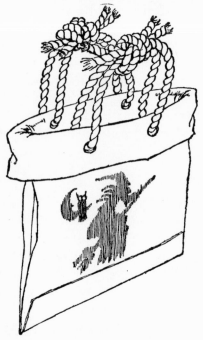

Roll down the top of the bag making four thicknesses of paper. Cut four pieces of heavy twine each 12 inches long for handles. Punch holes, 4 inches apart, on either side of the bag. Put one piece of twine through a hole. Pull it until the ends are even. Put another piece of twine in the hole 4 inches away. Pull it until the ends are even. Tie the four ends together with a square knot. Make a similar handle on the other side of the bag.

Decorate the bag. If a child can color within lines, draw a picture directly on the bag. Color the picture with solid color. Or draw a picture on a separate piece of paper. Cut it out. Paste it on the bag. There should be a picture on each side of the bag. Or make a "Snip-Snip Picture" (page 112) on each side of the bag. At Christmas time, the pictures might be a green tree and a big red stocking; in the spring, big tulips, or other flowers; for Halloween "trick-or-treat" bag, use witches, cats, or bats. A school or camp bag might be decorated with an assortment of colored circles, squares, and other forms.

Acorn-Top Jewelry

Materials: tops of two small acorns; bases for earring or pin; barley, rice, split peas, or glitter; household cement, shellac

Take the tops from two small acorns that are perfect and as near the same size as possible. Break off as much of the stem as you can. Sand the little nub that remains until it is flat.

There are several ways to decorate the earring. Put a little cement inside the acorn top. Sprinkle a little barley or glitter onto the cement. Let it dry a minute. Then shake off any excess. A more difficult project is to put a little cement in the center of the acorn top and place a split pea in the cement. Then put grains of rice around the pea like petals of a daisy. When the cement is dry, shellac the acorn tops, including the inside.

Put a drop of Duco cement on the base of the earring. Press the flat part of the acorn top into the cement. Do the same for the other earring.

PIN. Make a pin the same way, placing two or three little acorn tops in a row on the base of the pin.

Bottle-Top Boat

Materials: bottle top, bobby pin, paper, crayons, paste

Drop a bottle top into a pan of water with the cork side up. See

it float! Make a little sailboat with a bottle top bottom, a bobby pin mast, and a paper sail.

Cut a piece of paper 3 inches long and 1½ inches wide. Fold it in half to make a square. Cut from one corner to the corner across from it. Save the folded triangle. This is the sail. Throw away the other small pieces.

Slip the bobby pin over the triangle at the fold so that the closed end of the bobby pin is at the top of the sail and the open ends are

151

below the bottom of the sail. Paste the halves of the sail together. Stick the ends of the bobby pin into the cork in the bottle top.

Put the little sailboat into a pan of water. Blow gently. See the boat sail!

Wagon

Materials: small cardboard box, four ice-cream cup tops or four milk bottle tops, four two-prong paper fasteners, string, paints

Punch holes in the sides of the box where the wheels should be attached. Punch holes in the center of each ice-cream cup or milk bottle top. Fasten the wheels to the box with two-prong paper fasteners with the prongs opening on the inside of the box. Punch a hole in the center front of the box. Attach a string long enough to enable the child to pull the wagon.

Paint the wagon. If there is printing on the box, add one tablespoon of soap flakes to one-half cup of poster paint.

COVERED WAGON: Make a covered wagon which most children have seen on TV. Make a wagon as above. Cut a piece of white paper as long as the box and twice as wide. Attach the long side of the paper to the side of the box with two-prong paper fasteners. Attach the other side the same way.

TRAIN. Turn two or more small boxes up side down—two-pound processed cheese boxes are best. Use the top for one car and the bottom for another. Add wheels as above. See the box cars? Punch

152

a hole in the front end of the first car. Attach a long string. Fasten the other cars together with string. Play engineer and pull the train.

Puppet on a Stick

Materials: paper, light-weight cardboard, lath, thumbtacks, paste, crayons

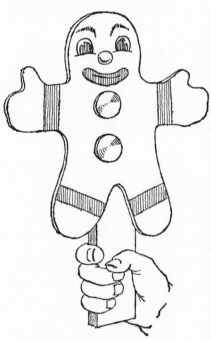

Color pictures of figures or characters in a song or story. They may be big figures, such as leaves or tulips mentioned in a song. Or they may be characters in a favorite story, such as the *Ginger Bread Boy* or *The Three Bears.*

Cut out the pictures and mount them on light-weight cardboard. Thumbtack the pictures onto a piece of lath or other small stick.

There are a number of ways that a child can play with these puppets. He can move a puppet up and down as he sings a song about the character. Or children can hide behind a table. As a leader tells a story, different characters may appear on the scene. Simplify the story so that no more than two characters appear at the same time.

Doll Bed

Materials: small cardboard box, such as candy box; eight identical spools, glue, paint, light-weight cardboard, cotton cloth, thread, old nylon stockings, embroidery floss

To make a leg of the bed, glue one spool on top of another. Make the other three legs the same way. Glue them onto the bottom of the box at each corner. If you want a headboard and footboard on the bed, cut them out of light-weight cardboard. Glue them in place,

153

holding the cardboard and the box together with snap-on clothespins while the glue is drying. Paint the bed.

To make a mattress, cut two pieces of cotton cloth 2 inches larger than the bottom of the box. Sew three sides together with ½-inch hems. Turn the tube right side out. Stuff it with old nylon stockings. Sew the top closed. Cut out sheets and blankets using pinking shears. Make a bedspread with fringe and embroidered with running stitch or cross-stitch (pages 123, 125).

Puppet on a String

Materials: construction paper, paste, string

To make this funny puppet you need seven pre-cut rectangles: one

piece 3 inches by 4 inches for the head; one piece 1½ inches by 3 inches for the neck; one piece 4 inches by 6 inches for the body; two pieces 1 inch by 6 inches for the arms; and two pieces 1½ inches by 8 inches for the legs. (To make a larger puppet, enlarge these dimensions proportionately.) Paste the pieces together to form a man. Cut out scraps of paper for eyes, nose, mouth, ears, and hair. Paste them in place.

Now, bend the arms up at the elbows, crease, and up the hands. Bend the legs up at the waist, down at the knees, and up at the feet.

Punch a hole in the center top of the head. Put a string, about 16 inches long, through the hole. Tie big knots in each end of the string.

Hold the puppet by one end of the string. Jiggle him up and down. Sing to him and make him dance.

The puppet may be bigger or smaller depending on the child's size and ability to handle a puppet on a string.

RHYTHM INSTRUMENTS

Use as many home-made instruments as you can for a rhythm band (pages 177-180). Making them gives a child an opportunity to construct something which can be used by different members of a group. A child may also make an instrument for himself and play it while listening to music. Making these instruments also offers an opportunity to combine a wide variety of handicraft skills: sanding, hammering, painting, pasting, sewing, and so forth.

Rhythm Sticks
Materials: dowel sticks, latex paint, crayons, or poster paint and shellac

Rhythm sticks may be made of dowels of various thickness; but they should be made in matching pairs. Saw dowels into 12-inch lengths. Sand the ends. Color the sides with crayons, using the flat side of broken crayons; or paint the sticks with poster paint and shellac; or paint with latex paint.

Beater
Materials: ⅛-inch dowel, glue, 1-inch round wooden bead or small rubber "jack" ball; or tinker toys

Dip the end of a ⅛-inch dowel into glue and force it into the hole of a 1-inch round wooden bead. Or sharpen the end of the dowel, dip it in glue and force it into the center of a small rubber ball—the kind used in playing jacks.

Bells
Materials: four small bells, elastic, thread

Cut a piece of elastic 1 inch longer than the distance around four fingers of the hand held together. Overlap the ends and sew the elastic into a loop that will fit over the four fingers. Sew little bells on one side of the loop. The musician claps his hands in time to the music, making the bells tinkle.

Tapper
Materials: paint paddle or 6-inch piece of lath, or "bolo ball" paddle; pop-bottle tops, two nails, paint

Sand the paint paddle or piece of lath or paint it. Remove the cork from the inside of some pop-bottle tops. Hammer the tin flat. With a hammer and nail, make a hole in the center of each top. Place one bottle top on top of another on the lath. Nail them loosely to the lath. The hole in the bottle top should be larger than the nail that holds them. Nail another set of bottle tops near the first set.

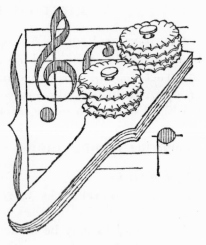

The rhythm-band musician holds the tapper stick in one hand and taps it gently against the other hand in time to the music. The metal pieces clang together with each beat of music.

Shakers Having a variety of types of shakers in a rhythm band produces a variety of sound effects. Using different kinds of materials inside the shakers and varying the amounts used also produces different tones.

Tube Shakers. *Materials:* cardboard tube; newspaper; paste; gummed tape; crayons or latex paint; rice, split peas, or beans

Use any kind of cardboard tube of any length; the inside of a roll of aluminum foil, paper toweling, or toilet tissue.

Cut strips of newspaper ½ inch wide and about 1½ inches longer than the distance across the end of the tube. Dip the strips into thin paste and cover the end of the tube with five layers of overlapping strips. Allow the paste to dry at least overnight. Put a small amount of split peas, dried beans, or rice into the tube. Cover the other end in the same manner. Color the tube with crayons or paint it with latex paint.

Ribbon-Reel Shaker. *Materials:* as above except empty ribbon reel instead of tube, heavy wrapping paper

Decorative ribbon often comes on reels with tubes which vary from 2 to 4 inches in length. Be sure that the ends of the reel are firmly attached to the tube before you use it for a shaker. Seal one end by pasting a heavy piece of wrapping paper over it. Put a few beans, split peas, or a little rice inside the tube. Seal the other end. Decorate.

Hummer

Materials: small comb, waxed paper, staples

Staple waxed paper around a small comb. Player hums a tune through the paper.

This is a melody instrument. Hummer may play alone or play in any rhythm band activity.

Drums Drums of different sizes and made of different materials have different tones when beat. One band might have a tin-can drum, nail-keg drum, oatmeal-box drum, and commercial toy drums. Drums can be struck with the flat of the hand or with beaters (page 155).

WOODEN DRUM. *Materials:* wooden nail keg, large, round cheese box, or wooden bucket; inner tubing; tacks; paint

Paint a wooden nail keg, large, round cheese box, or wooden bucket. Cut one piece of inner tubing large enough to fit over the top of the wooden container and extend about 2 inches around the sides. Place the tubing over the center of the container. Fold the sides down and tack in place.

CARDBOARD-CARTON DRUM. *Materials:* empty round cardboard carton, such as oatmeal box; paint; masking tape

Remove as much of the paper label as possible from the outside of the carton. Fasten the lid of the carton in place with masking tape. Paint it with poster paint or latex paint. The paint helps to hold the cover in place. Or decorate with Snip-Snip Cuttings (page 112), or cover with decorated paper (see index).

BONGOS. *Materials:* three empty round cartons of different sizes— such as a two-pound oatmeal carton, one-pound corn meal carton, or salt carton; paint; cord; paste

Remove the tops from the cartons and save them. Paint or decorate the cartons like Cardboard-Carton Drum (above). Decorate the covers separately.

Punch holes on opposite side of each carton, 3 inches from the bottom. Stand the cartons side by side with the largest one on one end of the line and the smallest on the other end of the line. Run a cord through the holes you punched, holding the three cartons together. They will stay in line as the musician in the rhythm band "bongs" first one and then another.

Sand Blocks

Materials: two pieces of soft pine about 3 inches wide, ¾ inch thick, and 4½ inches long; two pieces of wood about 2 inches wide, 2 inches thick, and 4½ inches long; coarse sandpaper; thumbtacks.

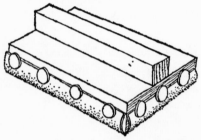

Saw two pieces of soft pine which are about 3 inches wide and ¾ inch thick into 4½ inch lengths. Sand them. Cut coarse sandpaper 1½ inches longer and 1½ inches wider than a block of soft pine. Place the block of soft pine in the center of the sandpaper. Fold the sides of the sandpaper over the sides of the wood. Cut out the extra paper at the corners. Glue the sandpaper in place, or fasten in place with thumbtacks. (The sandpaper will eventually wear out and need to be replaced.)

To make a handle, saw a 4½ inch length from a piece of wood about 2 inches wide and 2 inches thick. Sand it. Nail or screw it onto the uncovered side of the block of wood. (You can screw on old knobs from dresser drawers, if you have them.) Make the other block the same way.

A musician in a rhythm band brushes sand blocks together in time to music.

VII. Music

MUSIC REACHES RETARDED CHILDREN. IT "DOES THINGS" FOR THEM because it helps to fulfill many of their basic needs. Often the first means of communication with a retarded child is made through music. The mother sings to the baby in the crib, or in her arms. At last, he seems to recognize the voice and responds with a smile and perhaps a gesture. If the mother sings a song with simple motions, the child may imitate the motions and so join in the "singing" long before he can say a word. This joining in an activity with another person gives a child a sense of security, a feeling of belonging which can grow as he joins larger groups—the family, a group of neighborhood children, and later perhaps a class.

Singing is an expressive experience; people often express emotions through song that they may not otherwise be willing to show. Songs are happy, and sad, and solemn, and silly.

A family "singing-time," or "sing-song" brings about a feeling of oneness within that family, and is, therefore, a desirable addition to the day's activities. A goodly portion of the folk music that we all know, or should know, has simple unadorned melodies, strong rhythms, and words that are easy to understand, often repetitive, and is acceptable to all ages, children and adults alike. Many such songs could be included in the family repertoire.

In this feeling of belonging, there is an element of sharing. Everyone seems to enjoy music; and so a child who is singing or listening to music with others who enjoy it is surrounded by joy, in a sense wrapped up in a blanket of happiness. It is no wonder that we say a person is "wrapped up in his music" or "enraptured" by music. A retarded child easily becomes "enraptured" by simple, melodious tunes. This general feeling for music is contagious. It often catches the spirit of the retarded child long before anything else reaches him.

Because it is so contagious, the leader—whether parent or teacher —must make it clear that she, too, likes music. Teen-age retarded boys and girls often enjoy nursery-school tunes if they think that the adult whom they admire enjoys them. However, if a leader is condescending in his attitude and treats some tunes as "babyish," older boys and girls will copy the attitude of the leader and miss a lot of spontaneous fun.

Music not only gives a child a feeling of security when he is with another person or in a group; it also gives him a feeling of security and enjoyment when he is alone. A retarded child, when left by himself, may sing a tune over and over again; or seeing his reflection in a looking glass or in the shiny chrome on the dashboard of a car, may go through a motion song with his reflection while those around him are quiet. He may sing as he plays with his cars or with dolls. Many retarded children have collections of records which they enjoy playing when they are by themselves.

Music is a field for growth. The first tunes that catch the ear of a retarded child are very simple tunes with marked rhythm and usually simple words. A child usually learns to listen with his whole body; he sways in time to the music, claps out a rhythm, or uses motions as he sings a song. He can continue to like these simple tunes and still develop musically. Learning remains fun as he develops his ear for more complicated melody and develops his skill in responding to music with dancing and playing—first rhythm instruments and later melody instruments, and sometimes standard instruments.

SOCIAL DEVELOPMENT. Music may aid a retarded child in his social development besides giving him a feeling of well-being, happiness, and belonging; and at the same time stimulating him to learn to listen and respond. Self-control may be increased through singing in a group, by marching with others, and while playing rhythm instruments. When singing in a group, a child must wait for the signal to start; and if singing a motion song, wait for the right moment to make a motion. If marching, he must keep in line, and eventually in step, with others. If playing with rhythm sticks, he must wait for the right moment to join the music, and then accept the discipline of keeping time. He must also stop when others stop.

Singing to the end of a song increases attention span as does clapping out a tune or tapping the rhythm with sticks.

Music may also add to an appreciation of social concepts. These may range from general concepts of courtesy, happiness, love, and so forth, to more specific ones which urge a child to do socially desirable things such as brush his teeth and wash his hands.

Music adds greatly to a program of interest or study. A class interested in trains may learn to sing songs about trains, listen to the sounds of trains, move to train-like rhythms, as well as look at pictures and models of trains and pretend to travel on trains. Again, in using music this way, it must be fun first and educational second.

EMOTIONAL DEVELOPMENT. Music provides a release from tensions. When a child joins in a lively march or vigorous motion song, he works off excess energy. Often a lullaby, or other soft music, will calm him. A parent or teacher should always be sensitive to the needs of a child, sensing when to stimulate and when to calm him. When a child shows the first signs of fatigue, he should be encouraged to do something quiet.

PHYSICAL DEVELOPMENT: Any musical activity helps to develop a rhythmic sense which in turn aids physical co-ordination. Marching, gliding, "walking like elephants," or doing some other exercises to music develops large muscles. Taking part in some finger-play songs develops small muscles.

VOCABULARY. Singing helps to develop vocabulary and word meaning sense. Long before a child can say "finger," he can put his finger in the air at the correct place in the song and so identify his finger with the word finger. While singing certain songs, he may develop

161

concepts of "up and down," "in and out," and so forth. While singing old hymns and spirituals he may grasp general ideas, such as God's love. He may try to sing words with a group before he tries to say them alone because he is confident when he vocalizes with a group and self-conscious when he vocalizes alone.

CHOOSING MUSIC. Every child should have a variety of musical experiences. He should hear people sing, hear and see them play musical instruments, and listen to good phonograph recordings. It is impossible to list musical titles which young retarded children will enjoy, because a great deal depends upon an arrangement, the tempo, the accent, the key. This is especially true of records. You will recognize at once that some songs aren't suitable because they are too hard to sing—the range is too great, the melody too complicated, the words not meaningful to a child. You will find yourself feeling the same way about some records—too many words, words too difficult, not enough reptition, or tempo too fast. Other records will seem suitable at once. You will be doubtful about others and have to play them for the child to find out whether or not he likes them. When you find a record that "clicks," try to figure out what it has that a child likes. Your conclusions may aid you in making future choices.

Never be discouraged as you work with music with retarded children. Never dwell upon your own lack of musical ability. A simple song or record that "does something" to you is probably doing something similar to the child. A very severely retarded child may be absorbing more through music than his responses reveal. All retarded children need a great deal of music in their lives. See that they get it!

SONGS

Songs are more than music to a retarded child. They are a means by which he can express himself without having to form words of his own. He can express his mood—lively and gay or relaxed and pensive. He can vocalize before he can form thoughts of his own and put them into words. Saying "tap, tap, tap" for no reason except that a person feels like talking seems babyish, but repeating a word like "tap, tap, tap" in a song is acceptable.

162

Choose a variety of songs for a child to sing—some songs that are lively, some songs that are sweet and slow. Choose songs within an octave range. Choose songs which have words that are meaningful to a child—songs about things around him, about things he does or sees other people do, about attitudes he understands, such as "I love my doggy."

Whenever possible, supplement words with actions; they add meaning to words and aid greatly in speech development. They also aid a child, without his realizing it, to sense that his ability to think, his ability to speak, and his ability to act are all co-ordinated.

You can use songs which are primarily "action songs" and you can add action to songs which are not usually considered action songs. For example: point up in "Twinkle, Twinkle Little Star." Go through the rowing motions, using both arms, in "Row, Row, Row Your Boat." Rock a baby as you sing a lullaby. Fold your hands as if in prayer and rest your cheek on your hands in "Sleep, Baby, Sleep." Point to "you" and "me" when the words occur in songs. Give a sharp clap on the word "pop" in "Pop Goes the Weasel." Also sing songs that are definitely action songs.

Where Is Thumbkin? This very lively finger-play song is sung to the tune of "Frere Jacques." Singers wiggle their fingers one by one in the manner indicated below.

Where is thumbkin:	*(Put hands behind back.)*
Where is thumbkin?	
Here I am;	*(Bring fists forward. Wiggle thumbs.)*
Here I am.	*(Wiggle thumbs.)*
How are you today, sir?	
Very well, I thank you.	*(Wiggle thumbs.)*
Run away. Run away.	*(Put hands behind back.)*

(Repeat the song substituting second, third, fourth and fifth fingers for thumbkin. Wiggle all the fingers on the last verse.)

2. Where is Pointer?	*(Use index finger.)*
3. Where is Tall man?	*(Use middle finger.)*
4. Where is Ring man?	*(Use ring finger.)*
5. Where is Pinkie?	*(Use little finger.)*

163

6. Where are all the men?   (*Wiggle all the*
   Where are all the men?   *fingers and thumb.*)
   Here we are.
   Here we are.
   How are you today, sirs?
   Very well, we thank you.
   Run away. Run away.

VARIATION. Name the fingers, "Mother, Father, Sister, Brother, Baby." End with "the whole family."

The Clapping Song [2] This song has a variety of motions, and a change of mood. It starts with loud clapping, and ends with hands folded and eyes shut. *Children are seated. The words of the song explain the actions.*

The Clapping Song

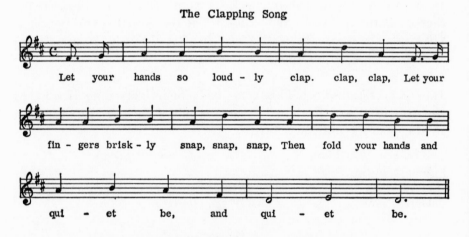

Let your hands so loud-ly clap. clap, clap, Let your fin-gers brisk-ly snap, snap, snap, Then fold your hands and qui-et be, and qui-et be.

Swiftly roll your hands so wide awake;
Let your fingers briskly shake, shake, shake.
Then fold your hands and quiet be, and quiet be.

Let us climb the ladder, do not fall;
Until we reach the steeple tall.
Then fold your hands and quiet be, and quiet be.

[2] Taken with slight variation from *Songs of the Child World Vol. 1,* Jessie Gaynor, The John Church Co., 1897.

The Fingers' Lullaby [1] This finger play is in a quiet mood, and ends with a lullaby. You can use the lullaby tune given here, or the traditional "Rock-a-bye Baby" tune.

Hold up the left hand. As you mention each finger, push it toward the palm with your right hand. When you sing the lullaby hold the clenched left fist in your right hand. Swing your arms back and forth in a rocking motion as you sing "Rock-a-bye baby."

The Fingers' Lullaby

[1] Taken with slight variations from *Songs of the Child World No. 1,* Jessie Gaynor, The John Church Co. 1897.

Five Little Chickadees[3] When singing a counting song, announce the number before each verse. Be sure that singers are holding up the correct number of fingers before you start to sing.

Five Little Chickadees

Harriet S. Jenks

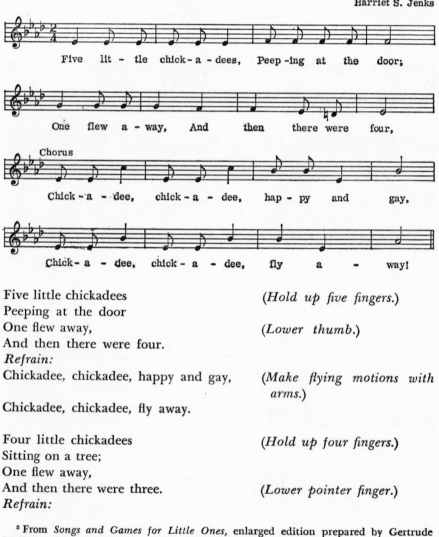

Five lit - tle chick - a - dees, Peep -ing at the door;

One flew a - way, And then there were four,

Chorus

Chick - a - dee, chick - a - dee, hap - py and gay,

Chick- a - dee, chick - a - dee, fly a - way!

Five little chickadees	(*Hold up five fingers.*)
Peeping at the door	
One flew away,	(*Lower thumb.*)
And then there were four.	
Refrain:	
Chickadee, chickadee, happy and gay,	(*Make flying motions with arms.*)
Chickadee, chickadee, fly away.	
Four little chickadees	(*Hold up four fingers.*)
Sitting on a tree;	
One flew away,	
And then there were three.	(*Lower pointer finger.*)
Refrain:	

[3] From *Songs and Games for Little Ones*, enlarged edition prepared by Gertrude Walker and Harriet S. Jenks, Oliver Sisson Co.

Three little chickadees	*(Hold up three fingers.)*
Looking down at you	
One flew away,	*(Lower middle finger.)*
And then there were two.	
Refrain:	

Two little chickadees	*(Hold up two fingers.)*
Sitting in the sun.	
One flew away	*(Lower ring finger.)*
And then there was one.	
Refrain:	

One little chickadee	*(Hold up one finger.)*
Left all alone.	
He flew away,	*(Close first.)*
And then there was none.	
Refrain:	

VARIATIONS. Children can act out this story-song in other ways. Five children stand in front of a group. Each one, in turn, "flies" to his seat at the appropriate time in the song. Or players form a circle with five children in the center. Each one, in turn, "flies" out of the circle, around it, and takes a place in the circle.

If You're Happy This song can be used as a sit-down song, using actions that require moving hands, head, and feet; or it can be used as a stand-song, using actions that require moving the whole body. You can use any type of action that will help the children to exercise. Announce the action before each verse. Sing to the tune, "She'll Be Comin' Round the Mountain When She Comes."

LEADER. Clap. Clap.
If you're happy and you know it, clap your hands. *(Clap, clap.)*
If you're happy and you know it, clap your hands. *(Clap, clap.)*
If you're happy and you know it,
Then you really ought to show it.
If you're happy and you know it, clap your hands. *(Clap, clap.)*

Other verses that can be sung while children are seated are:
Stamp your feet.
Wink your eye.

Bounce your seat.

Snap your fingers.

Bow your head.

Wave good-by. (Say "good-by" empathically at end.)

That's enough. (Say "That's enough!" empathically at end.)

Verses that can be used while children are standing are:

Turn around.

Touch your toes.

Jump up high.

Touch the sky.

Use verses to teach the parts of the body:

Touch your head.

Touch your ears.

Touch your nose.

Touch your chin, etc.

Also use actions found in "Mulberry Bush," "Wash your face," "Clean your ears" (page 189).

The Elephant Bending over and walking like an elephant requires using muscles that are usually neglected.

One child who plays the elephant, bends over with his hands clasp in front of him to make the animal's trunk, sways back and forth and walks around the group as children sing. At the end of a verse, he chooses another elephant. The song is then "two elephants," and so on. The group keeps singing until every-

one has had a chance to be an elephant—unless, of course, the group is large.

When every child is walking like an elephant, end the song with the line, "They called for another, but there was none."

Elephant Song

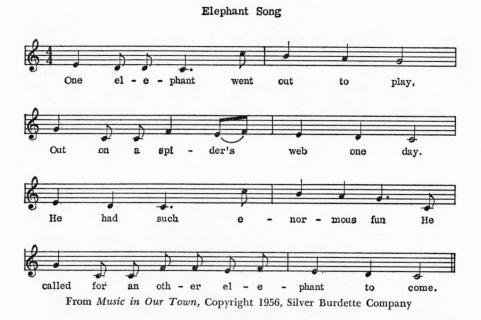

One el - e - phant went out to play,

Out on a spi - der's web one day.

He had such e - nor - mous fun He

called for an oth - er el - e - phant to come.

From *Music in Our Town*, Copyright 1956, Silver Burdette Company

Let Your Hands Go Clap Children stand in a circle or a line. The leader announces the action before each verse. Everyone sings the words to the tune of "Merrily We Roll Along" and does the actions indicated.

Touch your toes and then your knees;
Touch your toes; touch your knees.
Touch your toes and then your knees,
And let your hands go clap!

Touch the floor and stand up tall;
Touch the floor; stand up tall.
Touch the floor and stand up tall,
And let your feet go stamp!

169

Lift your foot and kick the ball;
Lift your foot; kick the ball.
Lift your foot and kick the ball;
And let your hands go clap!

Hug yourself and turn around;
Hug yourself; turn around.
Hug yourself and turn around,
And let your feet go stamp!

Lift your knee up in the air;
Lift your knee; in the air.
Lift your knee up in the air,
And let your hands go clap!

Stand on tiptoe, turn around;
Turn around; turn around.
Stand on tiptoe, turn around,
And let your feet go stamp!

Point your toe and take a bow;
Point your toe; take a bow.
Point your toe and take a bow,
And let your hands go clap!

Bend your body down and up;
Down and up, down and up.
Bend your body down and up,
And let your feet go stamp!

Rock your shoulders side to side;
Side to side, side to side.
Rock your shoulders side to side,
And let your hands go clap!

VARIATION. Have one child who performs well stand in front of the group and do the actions while the other children sing. This gives the child who can kick or stand on tiptoe a chance to perform. The other children have a chance to watch someone other than the leader demonstrate how the actions are done.

This Old Man This old folk song, which has various forms, lends itself to rhythms and rhythm band (page 177) activities, helps to develop rhyming and number sequence, and includes some dramatic action. It is available on records. This version gives a picture of an old man making music everywhere he goes.

Do not try to hold up the right number of fingers for numbers in this song. The music is too lively, and pausing to make sure that everyone is holding up the correct number spoils the fun and spontaneity. Clap on "Nick nack, paddy wack"; make a full-arm gesture on "everywhere," and point as indicated in the song.

Pause before each verse as leader speaks.

This Old Man

This old man, he played one he played nick nack,

just for fun, nick nack pad - dy wack

mus-ic in the air This old man played ev - 'ry where.

LEADER. One, just for—CHILDREN. Fun
This old man, he played one;
He played nick nack, just for fun.
Nick nack, paddy wack. Music in the air.
This old man played everywhere.

LEADER. Two, on my—(*Points to shoe.*) CHILDREN. Shoe.
This old man, he played two;
He played nick nack on my shoe. (*Point to shoe.*)
Nick nack, paddy wack. Music in the air.
This old man played everywhere.

LEADER. Three, on my—(*Points to knee.*) CHILDREN. Knee.
This old man, he played three.

171

He played nick nack on my knee. (*Point to knee.*)
Refrain:

LEADER. Four, on my— (*Pretends to knock.*) CHILDREN. Door.
This old man, he played four.
He played nick nack on my door. (*Pretend to knock.*)
Refrain:

LEADER. Five, on my— (*Hits his side.*) CHILDREN. Side.
This old man, he played five.
He played nick nack on my side. (*Hit side.*)
Refrain:

LEADER. Six, on my— (*Beats index fingers as though they were rhythm sticks.*) CHILDREN. Sticks.
This old man, he played six.
He played nick nack on my sticks. (*Beat sticks.*)
Refrain:

LEADER. Seven, up in— (*Points up.*) CHILDREN. Heaven.
This old man, he played seven.
He played nick nack up in heaven. (*Point up.*)
Refrain:

LEADER. Eight, on my— (*Swings back and forth.*) CHILDREN. Gate.
This old man, he played eight.
He played nick nack on my gate. (*Swing back and forth.*)
Refrain:

LEADER. Nine, on my— (*Taps spine.*) CHILDREN. Spine.
This old man, he played nine.
He played nick nack on my spine. (*Tap spine.*)
Refrain:

LEADER. Ten, on my— (*Points to boys.*) CHILDREN. Men.
This old man, he played ten.
He played nick nack on my men. (*Point to boys.*)
Refrain:

Found a Peanut Sing to the tune of "Clementine" and act this out.

Found a peanut, found a peanut, Found a peanut, just now; Just now found a peanut, Found a peanut just now.	*(Pick up imaginary peanut.* *Hold it up for all to see.)*
Cracked it open, cracked it open. Cracked it open just now; Just now, cracked it open, Cracked it open just now.	*(Clap hands on each "crack.")*
It was rotten; it was rotten; It was rotten, just now; Just now it was rotten; It was rotten just now.	*(Hold nose with fingers.)*
Ate it anyway; ate it anyway; Ate it anyway, just now; Just now ate it anyway; Ate it anyway just now.	*(Pop imaginary peanut into* *mouth.)*
Got a tummy ache; got a tummy ache; Got a tummy ache, just now; Just now got a tummy ache; Got a tummy ache, just now.	*(Rub stomach. Make face.)*
Call the doctor; call the doctor. Call the doctor right now; Right now, call the doctor; Call the doctor right now.	*(Dial with one hand; hold* *receiver with other hand.)*

Story ended. Story ended;
Story ended just now.
Just now the story ended;
Story ended just now.

This can go on to many improvised variations, such as:
Got a needle. Got a needle.
Operation. Operation.
Feeling better. Feeling better.

He's Got the Whole World in His Hands This old negro spiritual expresses God's love in terms that a retarded child can understand. Personalize it to include the people who are near and dear to them. If you have a small group, sing it until you have named everyone in the group. Announce the name or names of persons or things about which you are going to sing in the next verse.

He's Got The Whole World In His Hands

2. Mommy and Daddy
3. Brother and Sister
4. You and me
5. George and Janet (children in group or neighborhood)
6. Name of leader
7. Happy Day camp.

You can also use the words of the traditional song: fish of the sea; beasts of the field, birds of the air, wind and the rain, sun and the stars.

RHYTHMS

Rhythms are generally considered any actions to music, whether they are free and interpretive or more organized as in musical games, rhythm bands, or folk dancing.

174

Needless to say a child must have an understanding of rhythm, feel the beat of the music, before he can enjoy marching, let alone play in a rhythm band. He must also have a feeling of tempo—the slowness or fastness of music.

Obviously, he cannot respond rhythmically to music unless he really hears it; and to hear he has to listen, which requires a continuous development in all children. You can't just play a record and say, "Listen." A child must know what to listen for. He learns to listen, the old maxim says, so that he can listen to learn. If you can teach your child to listen to music, you can help him to listen to other things as well.

You must listen to the music with your child. He will watch your response and copy your reactions. A child must have considerable experience in clapping and tapping in time to music before he can try more organized activities of marching and playing rhythmic instruments. You can help build up this feeling for rhythm by singing songs such as, "If You're Happy and You Know It" (page 167) with its timed responses and "Pop Goes the Weasel" with a clap on the "Pop!" and by playing musical games such as, "Did You Ever See a Lassie" (page 184).

You do not have to be a musician to teach rhythms to children. Use the very simple tunes that anyone can sing. Or use records. A leader who is singing or using records (rather than playing a piano) can participate directly with the children, teach by example, and assist a child who needs help. He can give his total attention to the child or children, not dividing it with the instrument. If you think that music is fun, the children will catch your spirit. They are not concerned about your "tone quality," lack of range, or any other music deficiency which may worry you. Concentrate on giving music to the children.

Marching Retarded children love a parade, as do all children. Marching helps to fill a basic need without the child's knowing why. A retarded child becomes easily exhausted, espcially when he is concentrating on table work to his full mental ability. He easily becomes tense, irritable, and at odds with the world if he has to sit in one place too long.

The words, "Let's have a parade!" can be magic words if said at just the right moment before negative behavior sets in. They can also be magic words for a child who isn't subject to negative behavior but who likes the beat of marching feet.

One of the unique advantages of marching is that there is noise and action, and at the same time orderliness. There is direction; yet, in the play stage, there is opportunity for a certain amount of free motion.

When learning to march, parade around something, like a bench or a table. Without this directional object, children tend to mill too closely together; their movements are restricted.

In the beginning, give little direction. Let the children get the "feel" of the music; the beat of the march will increase the tempo of walking. When you think they are ready, give simple commands such as: "Stick out your chests!" "Hold up your heads!" "Swing your arms!" "Lift your feet!"

Types of March Music You can't go by name in choosing marches for retarded children. The suitability of a march depends upon the arrangement, its emphasis, the compelling effect it has—or does not have—on your feet. Listen for the drum's prominence, as this is what directs the feet. When you have selected a recording, try marching yourself. March with a child. Get the feel of the music before you introduce it to a group. Certain types of marches seem to suggest different actions. Some marches will be useful for more than one of the following activities, while others will be successful with only one.

PARADE. This type of music invites high stepping and marching with a baton. Give a child a rhythm stick to hold up high. See if he can pass it in back of him, from one hand to the other, and bring it to the front again.

MILITARY MUSIC. Pretend to be soldiers. Carry rhythm sticks like guns or flags. Play a stick like a horn or a flute.

RHYTHM-BAND MUSIC. There is a noisy kind of march music which suggests that marchers select a variety of rhythm instruments and play them in time to music as they march.

OTHER MARCHES. There is the type of march with a dominant

beat and pace that is irresistible and seems to encourage marching without action—except, perhaps, a salute to the flag in passing it. There are also marches which encourage marchers to chant—one, two, three, four or la-la-la-la.

Follow-the-Leader March Each child carries a rhythm stick. Children march in a circle. The leader calls out a command and demonstrates it as marchers pass in "review." For example, "Carry your gun!" "Play your flute!" "Wave your baton!" "Beat the drum!" "Blow that horn!" "Wave the flag!"

Playing Rhythm Instruments Most retarded children can learn to play and enjoy playing a variety of rhythm instruments. They can play them at home with favorite records or as they watch a favorite dance band or other musical program on TV.

Begin to develop rhythm band activities by using sticks only. Later introduce other rhythm band instruments, keeping one principle in mind. Keep the motion used in playing a clap-hand motion. For example, instruments that might appear to need only one hand, such as tappers, shakers, and so forth, should be held in one hand and tapped against the palm of the other hand or against another stick, held in the other hand. It is most difficult for retarded children, and all young children, to shake one hand in a rhythmic manner. The contact with the other hand establishes control and aids the child's co-ordination. It also enables him to make a more rhythmic sound.

You should acquire a number of records that have a compelling beat and vary in tempo and rhythmic pattern. As you work with a child, you will be able to tell from the rhythm of the tapping if the child hears the tempo and beat and senses that recordings differ.

Remember that this activity is tiring for most retarded children whose co-ordination is poor and small-muscle control is weak. Make practice periods short but frequent. Build up to a concert gradually. You and your child can make most of the rhythm instruments needed (pages 155-158).

Rhythm Sticks A pair of dowels (page 155) are tapped, one against the other, in time to music.

INSTRUMENTS UP! The game begins with the instruction. "Instruments up!" Everyone holds his sticks up or rests them on his shoulders. A player must play his sticks only while music is playing. When the music begins, everyone including the leader taps his sticks together in time to the music. When all the children are playing, the leader, without warning, lifts the arm of the phonograph. Everyone must stop playing. Make a joke about who wasn't listening and got caught. Praise children when they learn to stop at once. Play another record with a different rhythm and tempo. Repeat the game.

Other Instruments Encourage each child to play different instruments at different times in the rhythm band. You will get different sound effects, and each child will have a variety of experiences and use a variety of hand and arm motions.

TAP-CLAP INSTRUMENTS. A shaker, tapper, (page 156) and rattles of various kinds are all played the same way. The child holds the instrument in one hand and taps it against the palm of the other.

Wrist bells are played by clapping the hands together.

A child holds a tambourine in one hand and taps it with the other.

A child holds a triangle in one hand by a string looped over a finger. The triangle hangs free. The child taps the inside of it with a metal rod.

DRUMS. Small drums are held in one hand or on the lap and tapped with a beater held in the other hand. Play big drums by slapping them rhythmically with one or two hands.

SLIDE AND SLIDE INSTRUMENTS. Use cymbals only when marching, and then use them sparingly. Do not bang them together! Bring them to gether with a sliding motion with one hand going up as the other comes down.

Sand blocks (page 158) are rubbed together with a sliding motion with one hand going up as the other comes down.

Play Like the Leader The children watch the leader and do what he is doing with his rhythm sticks, in time to the music. The leader

may tap his sticks together, tap them on the floor, use them as a pretend violin, hold them aloft and tap them, tap his feet, and so forth.

After the players know exactly what they are supposed to do, this can be an elimination g a m e. The last player to follow the leader gives up his sticks. This may also be done with other r h y t h m instruments.

Sing the Beat When children have learned to clap well in time to music, have learned to handle their rhythm sticks while playing games and marching, and when they know a song with a definite beat, like "This Old Man" (page 171), they are ready to learn to play a song with sticks.

The leader says, "We are going to learn to play 'This Old Man' for the band. We are going to play it like this." He picks up his sticks and sings the tune of "This Old Man" using numbers instead of words (except for the few words placed in brackets below.)

1   2   3
This old man
1   2   3
He played one
1   2   3 (And)
He played nick nack
1 2 3
Just for fun

179

Sing the following words enthusiastically rather than singing numbers.
Nick nack, paddy wack
Music in the air.
  1   2   3
This old man
(Sang) 1 2   3.
        every where

Children then play their sticks, hitting them together, along with the leader singing, "1, 2, 3; 1, 2, 3"; etc. When they have learned to do this well, they may sing all the words and play at the same time. This is very difficult to do. New instruments may be substituted, or they may be used in combination with the sticks. You can eventually use other music which has a strong beat, but does not have words.

MUSICAL GAMES AND FOLK DANCES

Musical games and folk dances combine the fun of music with all its spirit-rousing sparkle and some of the fun of games—the acting together in certain patterns. The player senses the joy of being part of a group and gladly accepts leadership and conformity to rules. He learns to concentrate and act at the same time, to listen to the music and do what is expected of him at a certain time.

Through musical games, a leader may present a variety of physical activities which may aid the development of both large and small muscles. Musical games and dances are stimulating. They give a player a chance to work off steam; but a game should stop as soon as players show signs of fatigue. If one player tires long before others, he may be withdrawn from the game and asked to stand or sit near the leader.

Musical games and folk dances are group activities; but the group may be very small—a leader and two players. Sometimes a parent and child may sing the song of a musical game, acting out all the parts.

Music-Stop Games In music-stop games, players march, dance, or play a rhythm instrument in time to music and listen for the music to stop. Then, they follow a direction. It may be a spoken direction which requires a word-action concept. Or it may be a prearranged agreement to do some new action—which requires not only word concept, but a certain amount of memory work.

Freeze
Equipment: music

Players march in time to music. The leader stops the music. Players "freeze," stand perfectly still. At first, it may be necessary to say "freeze" when the music stops. Later the signal of the music stopping is enough.

There is no contest to this game; no one is withdrawn for not conforming. The object is to see if everyone can "freeze" at the right moment. If one player doesn't get the idea, he may be asked to stand beside the leader and watch the others. He may "freeze" in position, stand very stiff, when the music stops. Then he may again try marching and "freezing" when the music stops.

Squat
Equipment: music

Leader shows the players how to squat. Everybody tries it. Then they play the game.

Players march in time to music. When the music stops, they squat. Now, see who can squat first. Last person to squat after the music stops is withdrawn from the game and stands beside the leader. The game may be played until only one player remains. But it is often a good idea to stop playing after a certain time and tell the remaining players that they all do well.

Do as I Do
Equipment: music

This is a musical follow-the-leader game with players seated, without rhythm instruments, in front of the leader. The leader claps or taps in time to the music and the children imitate him. He may tap with the fingers of both hands his head, nose, chin, chest, shoulders, knees, toes, and so forth. When the children have learned to do it very well, in time to the music, they may take turns being leader.

181

Musical Chairs

Equipment: music, chair for each player

Chairs are placed in a circle. Each player sits in a chair. They get up and each player stands behind a chair. When the music starts, players march around the chairs. When the music stops, each player sits in a chair. Even when the children understand the game well enough to play it in traditional fashion, it is a good idea to go through this routine at the beginning of play. Then everyone has a chance to sit down when the music stops at least once.

When the players have learned to sit when the music stops, the leader removes one chair. This time when the music stops, everyone must scramble for a seat. One person will be left out. He will stand near the leader and watch the game.

The leader continues to remove a chair each time the game is played. At last only one player remains seated in a chair. Of course, he is the winner.

Singing Games In playing singing games, a group usually acts out a very simple story in time to a catchy tune. Often, but not always, a child plays a role and so is the center of attention for a few minutes. Often he can choose a partner which means making a quick decision while other players are held for a moment in suspense. A self-conscious child often loses some of his undesirable inhibitions as he is caught up in the group activity. There is lots of movement, and still everything must remain under control.

Most of the simple folk songs were developed to teach as well as to be fun. Actually they utilize the game technique to form associations between actions and words as well as associations between objects and words. These songs give opportunities to repeat basic speech sounds and give opportunities for exercise in basic physical movements that involve the use of large and small muscles. Most of these songs are adaptable to many purposes. But they must always remain fun!

Ring Around the Rosie Ring Around the Rosie seems to be one of the easiest singing games to teach. It is short, the tune is so simple that it is almost a chant, the count gives a sense of timing, and it ends with a definite climax—falling down, an experience familiar to all children.

Stress the meaning of the word "circle." Children usually find it easy to remain in a circle for this game because they do not drop hands until the last minute.

All join hands and go around in a circle singing:

Ring around the rosie,
Pocket full of posie.
One, two, three,
We all fall down! (*All fall down. Get up, and sing again.*)

Rig-A-Jig-Jig Rig-a-jig-jig may be played with players seated in a circle. One player is chosen to be It. It walks around inside the circle as everyone sings. The remaining action is described with the song.

Rig - A - Jig - Jig
English Folk Song

As I was walk-ing down the street, down the street,

down the street A lit - tle friend I chanced to meet, Heigh

o, heigh - o, heigh - o. Rig - a - jig - jig and a -

way we go, A - way we go, a - way we go;

Rig a-jig jig and a - way we go, Heigh o, heigh-o, heigh - o.

183

As I was walking down the street,   (IT *walks around inside circle.*)
Down the street, down the street,
A friend of mine I chanced to meet,   (IT *chooses partner. They go out-*
Heigh-ho, heigh-ho, heigh-ho!   *side the circle, join hands and walk*
around circle.)

Rig-a-jig-jig, and away we go,   (*Partners slide or skip, according*
Away we go, away we go.   *to their ability, in time to increased*
Rig-a-jig-jig, and away we go,   *tempo.*)
Heigh-ho, heigh-ho, heigh-ho!

(IT *sits down and partner becomes* IT.)

You can personalize the song by using the child's name.

As Jim was walking down the street, etc.
A friend of his he chanced to meet, etc.

VARIATION. Children may choose how they want to go down the street: skipping, running, gliding, and so forth.

Did You Ever See a Lassie? "Did You Ever See a Lassie" is played with players standing in a circle with one child in the center. Sing the child's name instead of "lassie" or "laddie." He enjoys the recognition. You will find that you can fit most names or nick-names into the song.

Did you ever see our Larry,
Our Larry, our Larry,
Did you ever see our Larry,
Go this way and that?

LEADER (*speaking*). Do something. (*If* LARRY *does not know what to do, or if the children have been repeating the first action each time the game is played, the leader may whisper a direction to* LARRY, *"Touch your toes. Clap your hands. Slap your knees. Hop around. Jump in place,"* and so forth.

Go this way and that way;   (LARRY *does action. Children imitate.*)
Go this way and that way.
Did you ever see our Larry
Go this way and that?

Larry chooses a new lassie or laddie. If the game is played in traditional fashion, pause before each verse and ask, "Is Mary a lassie or a laddie?" The children answer, "Lassie." Say, "That's right. Lassie."

Farmer in the Dell Some groups cannot stay in a circle, especially when they are learning a new song-game. This is especially true when they do not grasp each other's hands during the entire game.

It is easier to have children sit in a circle than to stand in a circle. You cannot play every circle singing game seated; but you can play a number that way, including "Farmer in the Dell."

Place chairs in a circle, one chair for each player. Players are seated. Call attention to the fact that they are sitting in a "circle." Choose one player to be FARMER IN THE DELL. He stands in the center of the circle. Everyone, still seated, sings:

The Farmer in the Dell,
The Farmer in the Dell,
Hi, ho! The derry-oh!
The Farmer in the Dell.
The Farmer takes a Wife.   (*He chooses someone who joins him in the center of the circle.*)
The Farmer takes a Wife.
Hi, ho! The derry-oh!
The Farmer takes a Wife.

(The song is repeated. The WIFE *takes a* CHILD. CHILD *takes a* NURSE. NURSE *takes a* DOG. DOG *takes a* CAT. CAT *takes a* RAT. RAT *takes a* CHEESE. *Each, in turn, joins the others in the circle. Then one by one they leave the circle as the group sings:*)

The Farmer runs away.   (*He returns to his seat.*)
The Farmer runs away.
Hi, ho! The derry-oh!
The Farmer runs away.

2. The Wife runs away, *etc.*   (*Returns to seat.*)
3. The Child runs away, *etc.*   (*Returns to seat.*)
4. The Nurse runs away, *etc.*   (*Returns to seat.*)
5. The Dog runs away, *etc.*   (*Returns to seat.*)

185

6. The Cat runs away, *etc.*   (*Returns to seat.*)
7. The Rat runs away, *etc.*   (*Returns to seat.*)
8. The Cheese runs away, etc.   (*Returns to seat.*)
9. There's nobody in the dell.
   There's nobody in the dell.
   Hi, ho! The derry-oh!
   There's nobody in the dell.

Terminating the game in this way avoids what may be a frightening experience—standing alone in the center of a noisy group.

Retarded children soon get the idea of "taking" Wife, Nurse, and so forth; but it is very hard for many of them to remember the roles they are playing and to return to their places at the correct time.

When they know the song well and have a concept of "circle," they can stand in a circle, join hands, and rotate as they sing the song up to the point where the FARMER takes a WIFE. They stand still as she joins him in the center and they finish the verse. They join hands and repeat the action for the other verses. They stand still as each of the characters runs back to take his place in the circle.

THE GOBLIN IN THE DARK. Once the children know the song, they can quickly learn a variation. It will be easier to teach the new version than it was to teach the song and game originally because the children already know the tune and are required only to learn the new words and actions. This is an example of moving from the known to the partially unknown in teaching.

The song is sung to "The Farmer in the Dell," but on a lower key, with a slower tempo, and with greater emphasis on the beat. Children sit or stand in a circle and act out the game in a scary manner. One child is chosen to be GOBLIN. He stamps around the inside of the circle, walking like a monster, as the children sing:

The Goblin in the dark,
The Goblin in the dark,
Hi! Ho for Halloween!
The Goblin in the dark!

The Goblin takes a Witch. (*He chooses a* WITCH, *who rides within the circle on a pretended broomstick.*)

The Witch takes a Cat. (*She chooses a* CAT, *who walks on all fours and meows.*)

The Cat takes a Bat. (*He chooses a* BAT, *who flies within circle.*)

The Bat takes a Ghost. (*He chooses* GHOST, *who stands very still with hand covering face.*)

The Goblin runs away, etc. (*He runs away.*)
The Witch runs away, etc. (*She runs away.*)
The Cat runs away, etc. (*He runs away.*)
The Bat flies away, etc. (*He goes away.*)
The Ghost says— (*Pause in singing*) Boo! (*He uncovers face to say "Boo!"*)

Leader Sings. The children run and hide, and so forth. (GHOST *covers his eyes with his hands.* CHILDREN *run and hide. At the end of the song,* GHOST *finds one who is the next* GOBLIN.)

London Bridge London Bridge is played in traditional fashion, with the exception that choosing is eliminated. Two children form an arch. Other players form a line, march under the arch, around one player, and through the arch again singing:

London Bridge is falling down,
Falling down, falling down;
London Bridge is falling down,
My fair lady. (*Players forming the arch drop their arms around the person who happens to be in the center of the arch.*)

187

Take a key and lock her up,	*(People making the arch and the*
Lock her up, lock her up;	*person in it rock back and forth.*
Take a key and lock her up,	*Other players stand still. All sing.)*
My fair lady.	

The player who is caught goes behind one of the players forming the arch and puts his hands on her waist. The game is repeated. The next player who is caught goes behind the other player forming the arch. After that, players who are caught join one line and then the other. The game continues until there are no more players to be "locked up."

Looby Loo In this song-game, the center of the circle represents a tub of cold water, just like the tubs of cold water in which families used to take baths once a week—on Saturday night. When playing, eliminate mention of "left" and "right," found in the traditional version. Say instead, "one foot," "other foot," "one hand," "other hand." It is hard for retarded children to learn directions. Of course, they should eventually learn "left and right" but it spoils the spontaneity of the game to stop in the middle of it and have the leader check to make sure that everyone has his *left* foot in at the correct moment. On the other hand, it is wrong to let a child make the mistake over and over again and so build up a wrong concept.

Two players may play Looby Loo, although it is usually played by a group. Players, including the leader, join hands and rotate in a circle as they sing the chorus. When they come to the verse, they stop rotating and each stands in place as he sings and follows the directions of the song, putting one foot in the circle, and so forth.

Looby Loo

Old Singing Game

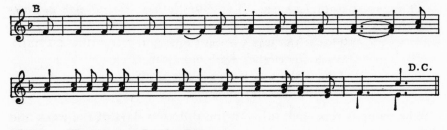

Chorus: Here we go Looby Loo,
Here we go Looby light;
Here we go Looby Loo,
All on a Saturday night.

1. I put my one foot in,
I take my one foot out;
I give my one foot a shake, shake, shake,
And turn myself about. (*Chorus.*)

2. I put my other foot in, etc.
3. I put my one hand in, etc.
4. I put my other hand in, etc.
5. I put one elbow in, etc.

6. I put the other elbow in, etc.
7. I put my head right in, etc.
8. I put my hip right in, etc.
9. I put my other hip in, etc.
10. I put my whole self in, etc.

Here We Go Round the Mulberry Bush "Here We Go Round the Mulberry Bush" is a singing game which may be played in traditional fashion; or it may be used to teach basic subjects. Or it may be used to encourage children to exercise in different ways.

The game has meaning for retarded children in its traditional form. The group joins hands and forms a circle. If the group is ready to learn the days of the week, the leader announces the day before each verse. Otherwise, the group sings, "So early in the morning" on the last line. The group stops between the two parts of the song as the leader announces the action to be pantomimed.

LEADER (*speaking*). Monday. (*Group rotates with hands joined, singing.*)

Here we go round the mulberry bush,
The mulberry bush, the mulberry bush.
Here we go round the mulberry bush,
So early Monday morning.

(*The group stops.* LEADER. *"Wash our clothes."* *Group pantomimes and sings.*)

> This is the way we wash our clothes,
> Wash our clothes, wash our clothes.
> This is the way we wash our clothes.
> So early Monday morning.

The game is repeated, substituting different days of the week and different actions.

Tuesday—Iron our clothes   Friday—Scrub the floor
Wednesday—Mend our clothes Saturday—Stir the soup
Thursday—Sweep the floor   Sunday—Walk to church

Use the game to remind children of things that they should do every day. Sing "So early in the morning," omitting the days of the week. Announce the action before it is time to pantomime. They sing "This is the way we: wash our face; wash our hands; shine our shoes; brush our teeth; comb our hair; zip our clothes; say our prayers."

Use the game to help retarded children to identify different parts of the body: Sing, "This is the way we touch our toes; knees; chest; head; eyes; ears; chin."

Use the game to utilize definite physical activity. Sing, "This is the way we: take a bow; hop around; nod our head; go to sleep; jump around; clap our hands; wave goodbye."

Of course, the order of action in the variations does not have to remain the same each time the game is played. When the children know the game well, the leader may point to a child before the time to pantomime. The child may call the action, "Wash your face," or some other action. The group will respond as directed.

Swinging in a Swing Players take partners. They join hands. This is the swing. In time to the music they swing their arms and bodies back and forth and sing:

Swinging In The Swing

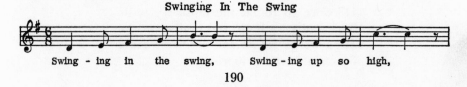

Swing - ing   in   the   swing,   Swing - ing up   so   high,

We can al - most touch our heads Up a-gainst the sky.

From *Social Games and Group Dances,* Elsom and Trilling, J. B. Lippincott Co., 1927.

When the players have learned the song and the swinging motion, divide them into groups of three. T w o join hands as they did before. A third player puts both his hands on one side of the "swing." If there a r e several players, all the third players face in the same direction.

The song is sung with the third player pushing the "swing" forward and back in time to the music. On the last word of the song, "sky," the "swing" is raised like an arch. The third player goes under the arch.

If there are several players, the "swinger" goes to the next "swing." The song is repeated. This game may also be played with three players, with each player having a turn to "swing."

Folk Dances Almost all folk dances must be simplified for retarded children who cannot be expected to learn complicated formations or intricate steps. Yet, they can enjoy folk dancing and react well to the music within a simple pattern. Some of them can develop skill as they have opportunity for practice.

191

Square Dancing Retarded children can dance square dances the same way whether the music is "Turkey in the Straw," "Skip to My Lou," or other square dance music. Use a recording which has no words.

Dancers choose partners. They do not form "squares" or other traditional formations. They are placed in couples around the room.

The LEADER calls and also dances, thus giving the dancers two clues for action—a clue they hear and a clue they see.
LEADER *calls:*

Bow to your partner	(*Dancers bow.*)
One hand	(*Each dancer takes the hand of his partner. They skip or rotate around.*)
Other hand	(*Partners change hands. Skip around.*)
Both hands	(*Partners grasp hands. Skip around.*)
One arm	(*Partners link arms. Skip around.*)
Other arm	(*Partners change arms. Skip around.*)
Bow to your partner	(*Partners bow.*)
Take your partner and follow me.	(LEADER *leads grand march around with sliding step.*)
Bow to your partner.	(*Partners bow.*)
And say thank you.	(*Partners say, "Thank you."*)

When the children know how to do this well, the leader can say, at the end of the dance, "Change your partners," and clap his hands. Everyone finds a new partner and the dance is repeated.

Mexican Hat Dance The music of "La Raspa," commonly called "The Mexican Hat Dance," seems to speak for itself. It is excellent for rhythm band activity as well as dancing.

The music in the first section seems to say, "We jump. We jump. We jump" and so forth. The music in the second section seems to say, "around, and around, and around," and so forth. It is all right for the children to jump, but the step is actually hopping from one foot to the other, extending the foot forward on the hop.

Children take partners. They hold hands on "We jump," and link arms as they go "'around and around and around." Another way to dance this is to form a circle.

VIII. Other Games

ORGANIZED GAMES DIFFER FROM OTHER ACTIVITIES IN MANY WAYS. Even the simplest game follows some rules, requires some degree of physical or mental skill, and offers some competition. This marks progression from singing games where the story-song, however vague, is important and the players perform in unison. As long as the group is orderly, the performance of an individual player in a musical game does not affect the group; and even when the player has a special part, as in "Farmer in the Dell," his role requires no skill.

In an organized game, a player either works for himself or for his team. His performance matters. In a simple game, like rolling a ball from one player to another, he receives praise for a good roll, and perhaps "too bad" if he doesn't do well. In more complicated games, an individual who performs well is an asset to his team.

Games have rules which are explained and enforced by a leader. Everyone in society must learn to abide by rules of acceptable social behavior and by laws which are enforced by leaders, or authorities. It is especially important for a retarded child to learn to accept authority; because, in later life, he will make few decisions for himself and the degree to which he is accepted by society may be determined largely upon his ability to conform to social behavior prescribed by authorities.

In teaching games, it is most important to discover what a child can do and go on from there. This avoids much frustration. For example: the program director of Happy Day Camp, run by the Raritan Valley Unit, New Jersey Association for Retarded Children, compiled the following figures. Of the fifty-five children attending camp on a certain day in 1957, all could walk, march, run, and gallop; forty-five could jump well, ten partially; twenty could hop well, thirty-two partially, and three not at all; twenty could slide well, twenty-five partially, and ten not at all; ten could skip well, twenty-five partially, and twenty not at all. Obviously games requiring marching, running, and galloping should be taught before games requiring skipping.

The director also found that of the fifty-three campers present on another day, fifty-two could roll a ball well, and one partially; thirty-three could throw a ball well, twenty partially; twelve could bounce a ball well, thirty-nine partially, and two not at all. A roll-the-ball game should come before a bounce-the-ball game.

Just as there is great variation in physical ability, there is variation in mental ability; and a leader must sense when a child is ready for a "don't tell" game or other games which require concentration and memory. Knowing just when and how to help a child to try something new without pushing him requires understanding of the total child. It takes patience.

Retarded children cannot follow complicated verbal directions of a game. A leader must show how it is played, demonstrating the directions as he talks. For example: "I'll roll the ball to Pete," as he rolls the ball to Pete.

At first a child may understand directions only partially; therefore he may soon lose interest in the game. This does not mean that the child cannot learn to play the game. Retarded children have to grow into a game, in a sense "be conditioned"; but once they have caught onto the routine of a certain game, they love being accepted into organized play and feel comfortable and safe acting within rules. They have the fun of doing something and the fun of being part of a group. Games help retarded children to express their personalities.

As a rule, retarded children accept competition. They learn to win or lose, either as a team or as individuals. However, they either win or lose each round of a game. Scoring means nothing to them and it really isn't necessary for young retarded children to try to build up the concept of scoring.

It is very important to alternate active and quiet games so that children may have a chance to "let off steam" and then relax. Through wise selection of a variety of games, a leader can help a retarded child to develop in all areas—physically because almost all games require some movement, mentally because players must remember some rules and routine and be alert for a turn, socially because the very word games indicates association of two or more people, and emotionally because a player is accepted by other people and because he has fun!

TAG

The first games of tag are usually completely unorganized games —a response to "You can't catch me!" These usually progress to tag games with rules. Everyone is free if he is touching base, or free if he is stooping, or free if he is touching wood. These loosely organized games may involve two players, or several players.

Free play may develop into a large variety of games requiring chase, and may be initiated when children are ready to perform as a group and have learned to accept rules. Players must know what is expected of them. Usually it is well to first walk through a game so that everyone clearly understands when he is expected to run, when he is safe, and so forth. Initial interest in a tag game may be very short; but as children gradually understand the game, their interest increases.

Vary tag games so that children will get exercise besides running. For example: "Drop the Beanbag" requires stooping and "Squirrel in the Cage" requires lifting arms. "Duck, Duck, Goose," encourages speech and listening for a cue.

Retarded children can't learn all the games that normal children play. Choose the ones that will help your group the most. Repeat the ones they like best. Stop an active game before anyone is overly tired or too excited.

Drop the Beanbag

Equipment: large beanbag

One player is given a large beanbag which will make a "thump" when it is dropped. Other players form a circle. The player with the beanbag walks around the outside of the circle. He drops the beanbag behind one player and starts to run around the circle. Leader and children call, "Tom, look at the beanbag!" (Of course, use the child's name.)

The player, behind whom the beanbag was dropped, stoops and picks up the beanbag. He chases the runner. If the runner reaches the empty place in the circle without being tagged, he is safe. If he is tagged, he stands in the center of the circle for one round. The player who picked up the beanbag now walks around the circle and the game is repeated.

The Monkey and the Peanut

Equipment: small object

One player is the MONKEY. He has a small object, like a wooden bead, which he calls a peanut. All the other children stand in a circle with their hand behind their backs.

MONKEY walks around the outside of the circle and drops the peanut into the hand of a player. MONKEY runs around the circle. The player who has the peanut chases him. If MONKEY reaches the empty place, he is safe. If MONKEY is caught, he is put into the Cage—the center of the circle. The player who has the peanut is now MONKEY.

Red Rover, Red Rover This game is played in a large room, such as a gymnasium, or an outdoor playfield. Several feet are marked off at each end of the playfield. Behind these lines are the safety goals.

One player is IT. All of the other players stand behind one of the goal lines. IT shouts:

Red Rover! Red Rover!
Angie (or whomever he chooses), come over!

Angie runs for the opposite safety goal. IT tries to catch her. If she reaches safety without being tagged, she stays there. If she is caught, she helps IT catch other players. IT calls the players, one by one, until everyone is caught.

The Piper Blows Tell the children the story of "The Pied Piper of Hamelin." Let them act it out in informal play. Then introduce this game which is based on part of the story.

Mark off an area, large enough to hold all the players. This is home. Everyone is safe in home. One player is chosen to be MOTHER, another to be the PIPER. All the other players are CHILDREN. MOTHER and CHILDREN are in the home. PIPER is outside.

MOTHER says:

I am going to the store to buy— (whatever she wishes.)
Here is a needle, now mend your clothes.
Pay no attention when the PIPER blows.

She pantomimes giving the CHILDREN needles. They pantomime sewing. She leaves, saying good-by, and so forth.

PIPER comes outside the house and either blows an instrument, or pretends to blow one. CHILDREN come out of home, get in line behind PIPER, and follow him as he walks around, blowing his pipe.

Suddenly, he stops playing. Everyone stands still. PIPER says, "Now, I'm going to catch you!" CHILDREN run for home as PIPER chases them. All who reach home without being tagged are safe. Those who are tagged must go with PIPER to the mountain, another area, where they remain as game is repeated.

MOTHER comes home. She asks, "Where are Pete and Sally (or whoever is missing) ?"

CHILDREN say, "The PIPER caught them." The game continues as before.

VARIATION. This game could also be The Music Man. The MUSIC MAN pretends to play an instrument as the leader plays a record on the phonograph. When the music stops, CHILDREN run for home as MUSIC MAN chases them.

Pom Pom Pull Away This game is also played in a large room or on a playground. Several feet are marked off at each end of the playfield. Behind these lines are safety goals.

One player is IT. All of the other players stand behind one of the goal lines. IT shouts:

> Pom pom pull away!
> Let your horses run away!

All of the players run for the opposite goal. IT catches as many as he can. All who cross the goal line are safe. All who are tagged join IT in the center of the field. IT calls out again. Everyone who is in the center field tries to catch the runners. The game continues until everyone ie caught or until the players are too tired to run anymore.

Duck, Duck, Duck, Goose! One player is IT. All the other players form a circle. IT runs around the outside of the circle, taps each person gently on the shoulder, saying, "Duck, Duck, Duck." He continues to say "Duck" until he suddenly taps a person and says, "Goose!" IT runs around the circle. GOOSE chases IT. If IT gets back to the vacant spot in the circle, he is safe. If IT is caught, he goes in the "basket," center of the circle. GOOSE becomes the next IT.

Cat and Rat One player is chosen to be CAT and another to be RAT. The other players form a circle and join hands. CAT stands outside the circle. RAT stands inside. The game opens with this conversation.

CAT. I am the cat.   (*Leader may have to say: "I am the ---"*)
RAT. I am the rat.   (*"I am the ---"*)
CAT. I will catch you.   (*"I will ------ ---"*)
RAT. No, you can't.   (*"No, you -----"*)

198

This is a signal for chase. CAT darts into the circle to try to catch RAT. RAT tries to escape him. Both may run in and out of the circle. The players in the circle raise their hands to help.

When RAT is caught, he chooses a new RAT. CAT chooses a new CAT. The game is played again. If, after a period of time RAT is still uncaught, the leader stops the game. The leader praises RAT for being a fast runner. He calls CAT a "Sleepy Cat" or a "Pokey Cat." New runners are chosen.

Squirrel in the Cage Players stand in groups of three. Two players form a cage by holding hands and standing as far apart as possible. The third player stands between their arms. He is the SQUIRREL in the cage. When the leader blows a whistle, each SQUIRREL must find a new cage. Other players lift their arms to let the old SQUIRREL out and to welcome a new SQUIRREL.

When players understand this part of the game, one player is chosen to be the SQUIRREL who has no cage. Other players form in groups of three, as above, making a circle around the lone SQUIRREL.

The leader must see that the cages are about the same distance apart so that SQUIRRELS will run equal distances when they change cages. The distance from the center, where the lone SQUIRREL is standing, to a cage should be about the same as the distance between cages.

When the leader blows a whistle, the SQUIRREL without a cage dashes for one of the cages. Each SQUIRREL darts out of his cage and tries to get into another as fast as he can. The players who are CAGES try to help their SQUIRREL to get out quickly. When a cage is empty, they call to other SQUIRRELS, "Come here!" The player who is left standing alone is the new SQUIRREL without a cage.

VARIATIONS. 1. If the children can talk, the lone SQUIRREL can give the signal for change. He calls, "Everyone look for walnuts!" Everyone changes as above.

2. Place a pile of beads or stones (one for each player) a short distance from the play area. At the signal for a change, everyone runs, gets a bead or stone, and then tries to get into a new cage.

Open the Doors! In this game, the leader gives the signal "Open the doors!" in consideration of the abilities of the children involved and with an understanding of the runner's need to win and be safe, or the chaser's need to win and catch.

One player is IT. Other players form a circle with their hands joined. IT walks around the outside of the circle. He tags a player. IT runs around the circle as the player who was tagged chases him.

Suddenly the leader calls, "Open the doors!" The players in the circle raise their arms to let IT pass into the house, the center of the circle. If IT gets inside the house before he is caught, he may stay there. Otherwise, he joins the circle. The person who was tagged becomes IT and the game continues.

The game continues until there are so many players inside the house that it is impossible to make a circle.

Peter Rabbit Here we have a story, which the children know well, turned into a game. One player is chosen to be PETER RABBIT and another to be MR. MCGREGOR. The other players form a circle and join hands.

The leader starts to tell the story. "One day Peter Rabbit was hop, hop, hopping around when he saw Mr. McGregor's garden. He looked at the garden. Then he hopped right inside. (PETER RABBIT *hops into the center of the circle.*) He saw a nice carrot, so he pulled it up and ate it. (PETER RABBIT *pantomimes story.*) He saw a radish, so he ate that, too.

"Now, Mr. McGregor came to work in his garden. He walked

around the outside. (MR. McGREGOR *walks around circle.*) He looked inside his garden. There he saw Peter Rabbit, eating a carrot and a radish. Mr. McGregor cried: (MR. McGREGOR *cries, "Stop, thief!"*)

This is a signal for chase. Mr. McGregor darts into the circle and tries to catch Peter. Peter tries to escape. Both may run in and out of the circle. Players in the circle raise their hands to help.

When PETER is caught, a new PETER and a new MR. McGREGOR are chosen. If PETER is not caught in a short period of time, the leader stops the game. He praises PETER for being a fast runner. He says, "Poor Mr. McGregor, are you tired or stiff today?" or makes some other remark.

BALL AND BEANBAG GAMES

It is easier to roll a ball than to throw one, and it is easier to throw a ball than bounce one. Therefore, it is a good idea to start teaching the use of a ball by rolling it from one person to another. At first there may be no direction, but gradually a child learns that he is expected to send the ball and to receive it. He may also build up word concepts of *from* and *to* and then from *me* to *you*, or to *Jim* or to *Mary*. Of course, this stimulates an association of words and actions. It establishes a purpose for direction and it also develops physical co-ordination.

A large, loosely stuffed beanbag is easier to toss and to catch than a ball. It also stays "put" when it is tossed. Therefore, it is easier to be accurate with a beanbag than with a ball. It it also safer to throw a beanbag indoors than a ball. Tossing underhand is easier and more accurate than throwing overhand. Children need to throw both ways.

Bouncing a ball and catching it requires considerable skill. But there is a special thrill each time a player succeeds. Because the activity does require considerable co-ordination and skill, don't try a group game involving bouncing until you are sure that each player can perform well.

All ball games and beanbag games start out as informal play. At first they involve two players. As times goes on, games may become more complicated. Many retarded children eventually enjoy many variations of baseball.

There are countless variations of games given here. Be on the lookout for ways to encourage a child to throw and catch. He has to use muscles which he will never use while walking or sitting.

Guard the Gate

Equipment: large ball

Players sit on the floor in a circle an arm's length apart. Each guards the space on both sides of him. Lift arms to fill the space—put up the gate, lower the gate.

When the children have the idea of guarding the gate, one player takes a volley ball, or other large ball. He rolls the ball as hard as he can across the circle, trying to get through an open space. Players next to the space try to stop the ball. A player who stops a ball may roll it across the circle.

If the ball goes through the circle, the two players next to the opening jump up and race for the ball. The person who gets it hangs onto it. Everyone gets in the position he was in at the start of the game. The person holding the ball rolls it hard and the game continues.

Praise the child who manages to roll the ball through the gates. Also praise a child who stops a ball.

Beanbag Call

Equipment: beanbag

Players form a line facing the leader. The leader calls the name of a player and tosses a large loose beanbag to him. The player tries to catch it and then tosses it back to the leader. Use an underhand toss.

Call Ball

Equipment: volley ball or other large ball

Children sit on chairs or a bench in a row facing the leader. The leader calls a child's name and bounces the ball toward the child. The child catches it if he can and bounces it back to the leader.

Bounce Ball

Equipment: volley ball or other large ball

When everyone can play Call Ball (above) well, play Bounce Ball with two teams. Teams stand in lines facing each other. The distance between the teams will depend upon the ability of the players. It is a good idea for leaders and more able players to stand at the end of the lines and in the middle to help all players get a chance to bounce the ball.

Players bounce the ball back and forth between the two teams. Scoring is not necessary. However, if the players have reached a point where they like to score, give a team a point whenever the ball passes through the opponents' line or when it stops bouncing on the opponents' side. Three points make a game. Play three games.

Keep It Up

Equipment: inflated balloon

Players form two teams which form lines facing each other. Place leaders and able players at the ends of the lines and in the middle in order to give everyone a chance to try to hit the balloon.

A balloon is tossed into the air. Players try to keep it aloft by hitting it back and forth between the two teams. Again scoring isn't necessary. But if players are advanced and wish to score, follow the rules for Bounce Ball (above).

Against the Wall Bounce

Equipment: Volley ball or other big ball

Players sit on chairs or a bench in a row on one side of the playroom. The leader throws a ball against the opposite wall and calls a child's name. The child runs up and tries to catch the ball after the first bounce. He bounces the ball back to the leader and takes his place in line again.

Knock Them Down

Equipment: five empty milk cartons, big beanbag, wooden beads

Practice throwing a beanbag overhand. Line five empty milk cartons up on a bench. A player stands a few feet away from the bench and in front of it. He sees how many cartons he can knock

203

over in three throws. He receives a bead for each carton he knocks over.

Players take turns. See who has the most beads after everyone has had his turn. If players are still interested, have everyone throw again. Count the beads again.

Bowling

Equipment: ten clean empty milk cartons, large ball, beads

Set up clean empty milk cartons like tenpins. A player stands a few feet away. He rolls the ball and sees how many cartons he can knock over. He receives a bead for each carton.

Set up the cartons again. The next player rolls the ball. When every player has had a turn, each counts his beads again. Who has the most?

VARIATION. Play with fewer cartons. Set them up one behind the other. See if a player can make them tumble over with one roll of the ball.

Ping-Pong Ball Blow

Equipment: ping-pong ball or piece of tissue paper crumpled into ball

Place the ball in the center of a table. Players stand on opposite sides of the table. At a signal, everyone tries to blow the ball off the opposite side of the table. Play as long as everyone is interested and not too tired. Keep score only if players are advanced enough to care about scoring. Count five wins a game.

Stride Ball

Equipment: large ball

One player stands with his feet apart. Another player tries to roll a large ball between the legs of the first player. They take turns.

When the players have learned to roll accurately, the first player tries to roll the ball between the legs of the second player. The second player tries to stop the ball with his hands. They take turns.

Circle Stride Ball

Equipment: large ball

When the players know how to play Stride Ball (above), they are ready for a group game. One player has a large ball. Other

players stand in a circle around him. They stand in a stride position with feet touching. Feet must be kept in this position while the ball is in play.

The player in the center looks around the circle to make sure that all feet are touching. He then tries to roll the ball outside the circle between the legs of a player. The player tries to stop the ball with his hands. He must keep his legs spread apart.

If a player stops a ball with his hands, he may go in the center. If the ball goes outside the circle, the player who missed it gets it and rolls it back to the center player. Players in the circle again take the stride position. After he has checked to see that all feet are touching, the center player rolls the ball again. If the ball goes outside the circle three times, the center player chooses another player to be in the center.

Toss on a Picture

Equipment: beanbag, cardboard squares, pictures

Cut several pieces of cardboard, such as shirt boards, into 8½-inch squares. Paste a magazine picture on each square. These may be pictures of general interest, such as animals and things to eat, or

205

they may be pictures that fit into a category, such as things in the kitchen: stove, sink, refrigerator. Include some pictures which start with letters that are hard for certain children; if a child finds it hard to say "s" include soap and a saw.

Place the squares on the floor, picture side down. Child tosses a beanbag, underhand, and wins any picture that the beanbag touches. The leader asks the child, "What did you win?"

The child says, "A car," or whatever it happens to be, and shows the picture to the class.

What Do You Need? This time choose pictures that form a complete group. For example: "We are going to try to get a sandwich. We need bread *(show picture of bread)*, meat *(show picture)*, and butter *(show picture)*."

Have one picture of each type for each player. Cards do not need to be identical, but each player should be able to get three cards. Place cards on floor, picture side up. Child must figure out what he needs and toss accurately in order to win the right picture.

You do not have to have groups of three and you can choose any number of subjects:

Get dressed: shoes, socks, dress or suit

Take trip: car, suitcase

Brush teeth: toothbrush, tooth paste

Furnish bedroom: bed, dresser, chair

When the child has played this way for some time, turn the pictures over. If a child gets what he needs, he may keep it. Otherwise, he sets it down on the floor again, face down. Keep playing until everyone has all the cards he needs to complete his set.

Number Toss

Equipment: wrapping paper, beanbag, beads, or other small objects

This game is helpful for beginning number work. Using a heavy black crayon, rule a large piece of wrapping paper into eight sections. In each section, write one number from 0 up through 3. It is very important for children to realize that 0 means nothing. Draw forms

in each section to represent the number indicated. For example: on 2, draw two bugs.

Place the wrapping paper on the floor. Near it place a box containing a number of beads, plastic toys, or other small objects. Give a child a beanbag. Have him stand in front of the wrapping paper, and a few feet away from it, and toss the beanbag underhand onto the paper. Ask him what number he got. (The leader must decide if the beanbag is on one square or another.) Tell him to take that many beads out of the box. Ask the other children how many beads Billy (or whoever threw) can have. Give him nothing if the beanbag does not land on the paper. If it lands on 0, talk about the meaning of zero.

Each player has three tries, and then another player throws. If you wish, keep score on a blackboard as well as with the beads. Have children count as you write.

DON'T TELL AND GUESS WHAT

In Don't-Tell games, someone or several players know a secret which must be kept from someone else. They know who did something, what object was chosen, or what made a certain noise. It is very, very hard for retarded children to keep a secret. Not telling requires a great deal of self-discipline.

Guess-What games require the use of senses. A player feels or hears something and guesses what it is.

Many of these games also help a child to form an association between words and objects, or between words and action. They require concentration and help to increase the interest span.

Who Said That?

Equipment: blindfold

One player is blindfolded. He stands with his back to the group. The leader points to someone in the room who says, "Hi!"

The leader asks, "Who said that?"

The blindfolded child answers, "Paul" (or whatever the name is) if he recognizes the voice.

If the blindfolded child cannot speak, the leader says, "Show me who said that." The child goes to the person whom he thought spoke.

A player may try twice to guess a voice, and then a new IT is chosen. After the children have played the game for a period of time, they will not need to be blindfolded. The leader makes sure that IT is facing where he cannot see who is speaking.

Which Hand?

Equipment: pebble, piece of paper, or other small object

This game can be played almost any place—while waiting for a bus, while resting in the shade, or after an active game in a playroom. It is one of the first games that severely retarded children can play with each other without direction or constant supervision. There may be two players or a small group.

IT has a pebble or or a piece of paper, or anything small. He puts his hands behind him and closes his fists over the object. He presents both clenched fists to a guesser who taps one. If the object is in that hand, IT must give it up. The guesser becomes IT, and the game is played as before. If the guesser guesses incorrectly, IT puts his hands behind his back again. He may shift the pebble to the other hand, or he may keep it in the same hand. He again presents his hands for guessing. If there are several players, he chooses someone who hasn't had a turn to guess.

Teacher

Equipment: Stone or other small object

This game is traditionally played on steps. One or more children sit on the bottom step. TEACHER stands in front of them. She has a stone or other small object in her hand. She puts her hands behind her and shifts the stone. Then she closes her fists tight and stands in front of the first child. She extends her fists and asks, "Which hand has the stone?"

The child points to one hand and says, "This one." TEACHER opens her palms. If the child guessed correctly, he goes up one step. If he guessed incorrectly, he stays where he is.

TEACHER moves on to the next child. She again puts her hands behind her and shifts the stone. Of course, she may keep it in the same hand or change it to the other. She repeats the performance with the second child.

The game is repeated until one child reaches the top step. He is then TEACHER. If a child cannot speak, his pointing to the hand is accepted. If he is TEACHER, he may extend his hands without asking the question. He will get the exercise of opening and closing his hands and enjoy the suspense that always comes with wondering if a person is going to guess right or wrong.

If there are no steps, a child may move back a little. Four moves will take a player to the "top of the steps." Or have a box of small objects. Give an object to a player each time he guesses correctly. First player to have four objects wins.

Warm, Hot, or Cold?

Equipment: jar of hot water, jar of cold water, jar of warm water, blindfold

Fill a jar with cold water—very cold with ice cubes in it. Fill another jar with warm water. Fill a third jar with water as hot as you can stand to hold it without burning yourself. Let everyone feel the jars. Practice telling which is hot, which is cold, and which is warm. Then play a game.

Blindfold one player. Choose a jar. Let everyone who is not blind-folded feel the jar and not tell if it is hot, warm, or cold. Ask the blindfolded player, "Do you think I have the warm jar, the hot jar, or the cold jar? Which jar do you think I have?"

The blindfolded player guesses. He then feels the jar. The leader asks, "Were you right? Is it hot? (or cold or warm?)" Blindfold another player.

What Noise Was That? One player is IT. He is blindfolded. The leader makes a noise. He may knock one block off a pile, bang the wastebasket, strike a note on the piano, or make a noise with a rhythm instrument. IT tries to guess what the noise is. Other players may not give away the secret, but they may tell IT if he is right or wrong.

What Is He Doing? Retarded children like to pantomime a simple act. The leader says, "Carl is playing. Guess what he is doing." Carl then pantomimes throwing a ball, or fishing, or any other simple act. Others guess what he is doing. Players take turns.

If a child is not sure what he wants to do, the leader may whisper something in his ear. If all the children want to do the same thing, he may whisper a new idea in the ear of the actor. Sometimes an actor may want to whisper into the ear of the leader before he acts. He feels more confident if he has the leader's approval.

What Is It?

Equipment: large bag containing object without sharp edges for each player

Put a number of objects without sharp edges in a big bag—a pencil without a point, a bead, a block, a bobby pin, a mitten, and so forth. Have at least one object for each player.

The leader holds the bag in front of a player. He puts his hand into the bag without looking. He takes hold of something and tries to guess what it is. He pulls it out of the bag. Did he guess correctly? The next player has a turn.

What Is Missing?

Equipment: tray, four or five objects

Place four or five objects on a tray—a paper cup, a crayon, a pencil, a bead, and a block, or other objects. Give everyone a chance to look at the tray and to name the objects out loud.

One player is IT. He goes across the room and stands facing the wall, his back to the group. The leader takes away one object. No one must tell what is missing. IT returns. He tries to name what is missing. The group tells him if he is right or wrong.

WHO HAS IT? Sometimes a player withdraws an object instead of the leader's doing it. Everyone puts his hands behind his back. IT names what is missing, then tries to guess who has it. After each guess, the player shows his hands. If they are empty, IT guesses again. He may have three guesses, then whoever has the object shows it. Another IT is chosen.

Blindman's Buff

Equipment: blindfold

Players are seated in a circle. One player is blindfolded. Players in the circle change positions. BLINDMAN turns around three times. He walks until he comes to a player. He touches him and tries to guess who he is. Other players must not tell.

The blindfold is removed. Did BLINDMAN guess correctly ?Another player is blindfolded and the game is repeated.

This game may also be played standing if there are no objects in the room over which BLINDMAN can stumble. It is not necessary for players to stay in a circle. However, they must stand still after they have changed places.

Guess What It Is

IT and the leader confer about something to guess. Perhaps they decide on ice cream and then choose a flavor. They go back to the group. IT sits down in front of the group. The leader says, "Harry (or whatever the child's name is) went to a birthday party and had something good to eat. Can you guess what it is?"

Each player guesses in turn. It is hard not to call out of turn. A child may guess cake. The leader says, "Harry, is it cake?"

Harry says, "No." When children know the game well, they may be able to answer without the leader's prompting. The leader may have to give clues to help the guessers. He may say, "It was cold." "It melts if it gets hot."

If a player guesses ice cream, the leader then asks, "What flavor?" The player who guesses the correct flavor becomes IT.

The leader always gives a little clue before the new games starts. "Sally went to the store and bought a toy." "Tom went to a farm and saw an animal." "Kate sang her favorite song." "Ralph played his favorite game." Obviously, the thing to be guessed must be

211

within the children's experiences. Encourage recall on class activities. Try to get children to think of outside experiences that are common to all children.

We Are Thinking of Something The game is played in a large room or on a playfield. Safety goals are marked off on each end of the playfield. Players are divided into two teams. One team thinks of something in a certain category as in Guess What It Is (page 211).

Players meet in the center of the room. The opposite team tries to guess what the first team has choosen. When someone guesses correctly, the first team runs for its goal line. The guessers chase them. All who are tagged join the opposite team. The opposite team then chooses something.

RELAY RACES

Taking part in a relay race requires considerable mental, physical, and social development. A player must be able to remember a chain of events. Usually he waits for a signal to start, or waits for his turn, he runs, he performs an act, he returns to his team, tags the next player, then goes to the end of the line. This is a big order and going through the routine is a triumph regardless of the outcome of the race.

Relay races aid social development because players must have a sense of taking turns, a feeling for a team, and each player must be able to perform while people are cheering for him—or for someone else. If he "goofs" when it is his turn, he must be able to take the criticism.

Obviously, each player must understand the expected routine and must be able to do everything that is required—jump, throw, or whatever the race involves. It is a good idea to walk out a relay, or pass the ball, or do whatever is expected before the race is run. Always give each player a chance to perform—even if one team has won a race.

Each race is won or lost. There is no need to keep score. If a race is repeated, change the order of racing so that the same players don't always run first, leaving players on the losing team to go through the routine without a contest each time.

Relay races described here are a sample of the large variety of races which retarded children may enjoy. They illustrate how many physical movements may be combined with walking and racing— jumping, toting, passing, lifting, blowing, and so forth. In fact, there is scarcely any skill that cannot be utilized and strengthened in some form of relay race.

Beanbag Relay

Equipment: large, flat beanbag for each team

Teams line up single file behind leaders. Each leader is given a large, flat beanbag which he places on his head. Players are warned not to touch the beanbag while they are racing! At a signal, leaders walk, or run, across the room, touch a wall, and return to their teams. If a runner drops a beanbag, he must stop, put it on his head, and continue. The leader gives the beanbag to the next in line who repeats the performance. First team to have each member run and return to the team wins. The race continues until each player has had a turn to run with the beanbag on his head.

Pass the Ball Relay

Equipment: large ball for each team

Players form relay teams. Teams line up single file behind leaders. Each leader is given a large ball. Players assume a stride position. At a signal, the leader of each line passes the ball between his legs. Each player in turn receives the ball and passes it down the line. The last player picks it up, runs to the head of the line, and repeats the performance. First team to get back to its starting position wins. Each player must have a chance to start the ball down the line.

VARIATIONS. Pass the ball overhead. Or have players of each team line up side by side, all facing the same direction. The leader hands the ball to the person next to him who passes it down the line. Race continues as above.

Spoon Relay

Equipment: tablespoon and small object for each team

Teams line up single file behind leaders. Each leader is given a

213

tablespoon and some object that will fit into it—a small potato, peanut, or block. The leader puts the object into the spoon. He must carry the spoon by the handle and he must not let it touch his body as he walks.

At a signal, each leader walks to the opposite wall, touches it with his free hand, turns around and returns to his team. If he drops what he is carrying, he must pick it up and put it in his spoon again.

The leader gives the spoon and the object to the next in line who repeats the performance. The team which gets back to its original position first wins. But the race continues until each player has had a chance to walk with the spoon.

Blow Them Over Relay

Equipment: stand-up paper figures (page 44), chair for each team

Teams line up on one side of the room behind leaders. On the opposite side of the room, place a chair in front of each team. On each chair place three or five paper figures (page 44).

At a signal, each leader runs to the chair in front of his team, puts his hands behind his back, and blows the figures off the chair. He picks them up, stands them on the chair again, and returns to his team. He tags the next in line who repeats the performance.

The team which finishes first wins. But every player must have a chance to blow the figures off the chair and stand them up again.

Up and Down Relay

Equipment: an old inflated inner tube, or a circle drawn on the floor or ground for each team; three upright objects for each team.

These may be empty milk cartons, rectangular blocks, Indian clubs, or empty cones that are obtainable from knitting mills. The last are easy to store, one on top of the other, when the race is over.

Two teams line up single file behind leaders. In front of each team, but on the oposite end of the playroom, place an old inflated inner tube. Inside each inner tube, place three empty milk cartons —or one of the objects mentioned above.

The teacher stands between the two teams, and during the race constantly calls directions and stimulates enthusiasm.

At a signal, the first runner of each team runs to the inner tube in front of his team, knocks over all the milk cartons, runs to the teacher, shakes his hand, returns to the inner tube, sets the cartons upright, and returns to his team. He taps the hand of the next player who repeats the performance. First team to have each member go through this routine wins. However, the race continues until each player has had a turn.

Out and in Relay

Equipment: an inflated inner tube for each team; three empty milk cartons for each team, or other objects see above

The equipment and the set-up is the same as for Up and Down Relay (above). Players line up in teams in single file, facing the inner tubes. At a signal, the first player on each team runs to the tube in front of his team, takes the milk cartons out of the center of the tube and places them upright near the tube. If a carton topples over, the player must return and set it upright. The runner returns to his team and tags the next in line.

The second runner sets all the cartons upright inside the tube and returns to his team. The race continues until each runner has either placed the cartons in or out of the tube. First team to have everyone perform wins.

Tin-Can Tower Relay

Equipment: four tin cans of graduated sizes, with smooth edges— one set for each team (a frozen juice can, soup can, No. 2 can, and No. 2½ can) ; an old inflated inner tube for each team, or a circle drawn on the floor or ground for each team

Set inflated inner tubes, several feet apart, in a straight line at one end of the playing space. Have one inner tube for each team. If you do not have inner tubes, draw circles 3 feet in diameter.

In the center of each circle, place four tin cans of graduated sizes, one on top of the other like a tower. Players line up in teams single file facing the inner tubes. At a signal, the first player runs to the inner tube in front of his team, knocks down the tower, and builds it up again, *outside* the inner tube. He returns to his team and taps the next in line.

The second runner knocks down the tower and builds it *inside* the inner tube. He returns to his team and the race continues until every player has had a chance to knock down a tower and build it again. The team to first have all of its members perform wins.

Nested Tin-Can Relay

Equipment: same as Tin-Can Tower Relay (above)

This race is run like Tin-Can Tower Relay except that the tin cans are nested inside the inner tubes. The first player on each team takes them apart, sets them outside the inner tube, and nests them again. The next runner on each team takes them apart, sets them inside the inner tube and nests them again.

Clothesline Relay

Equipment: clothesline; clothespin, rag or sock for each player; two pans for each team

A clothesline is strung across one end of the playing space. It should be about shoulder high for most of the players.

Players form teams and line up single file facing the clothesline. In front of each team, and under the line, are two pans: one holding a clothespin for each player, and the other holding a rag or sock for each player.

At a signal, the first player of each team runs to the line, hangs a rag or sock on the line using a clothespin, returns to his team, and taps the second player who then repeats the action. If any wash falls off the line, the player who is running for his team must hang the wash up again before another player may run.

The game continues in relay fashion. First team to hang all its

216

wash on the line wins. However, each player must hang up his wash.

CLOTHESPIN SNAP. If it is not convenient to have a clothesline, stand a large carton in front of each team. Have each player snap a clothespin onto the edge of the box instead of hanging up wash.

Blow It Along the Line Relay

Equipment: paper figure for each team; string 36 to 40 inches long strung between two chairs for each team

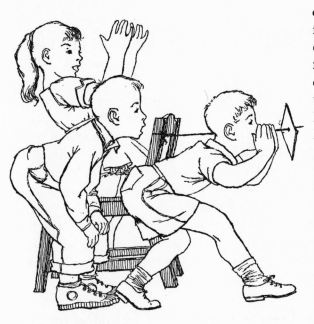

Cut out an interesting paper figure for each team; for example, a star, flower, or geometrical figure—any figure as wide as it is high. Punch a large hole, bigger than a piece of string, in the center. Put the figure on a piece of string 36 to 40 inches long. Tie the ends of the string to two chairs. Place the chairs so that the string is taut. Move the figure to end of the string. Put a figure on a string, in this manner, for each team. Children should have a lot of practice blowing a figure from one end of the string to the other before they have a race.

For a relay race, players line up behind leaders single file. At a signal, each leader runs to the chairs in front of his team, blows the figure across the string to the other end, returns to his team, and tags the next in line. He blows the figure back across the string. First team to have every member blow the figure across the string wins. However, every player must have a turn to blow.

217

BOOKS AND PAMPHLETS THAT MAY HELP YOU

A MORE COMPLETE LISTING of books and pamphlets dealing with mental retardation may be had by writing to the National Association for Retarded Children, 386 Park Avenue, South, New York, New York and requesting "A Basic Library on Mental Retardation," cost ten cents. The national office also has listings of books and pamphlets in special fields, such as welfare work, nursing, and so forth, which will be sent upon request.

Listed below are some books and pamphlets that many teachers and parents have found helpful. Some are written for all young children; others are concerned solely with mentally retarded children. We have presented our limited listing in two areas.

I. Books and pamphlets that may present you with ideas for projects and training.

Act It Out. Bernice Wells Carlson. Nashville: Abingdon Press, 1956.

American Folk Songs for Children. Ruth Crawford Seeger. New York: Doubleday and Company, Inc., 1948.

Can You Guess? Leonore Klein. New York: Wonder Books, 1953.

Finger Play and Action Rhymes. Frances E. Jacobs. New York: Lothrop, Lee and Shepard Co., Inc.

Fun for One or Two. Bernice Wells Carlson. Nashville: Abingdon Press, 1954.

I Can. Helen G. Schad. New York: Wonder Books, 1958.

Kindergarten in the Kitchen. Polly Culbertson. Dunlap Printing Co.

Make It and Use It. Bernice Wells Carlson. Nashville: Abingdon Press, 1958.

Make It Yourself! Bernice Wells Carlson. Nashville: Abingdon Press, 1950.

More Songs to Grow On. Beatrice Landeck. St. Louis: William Morrow and Co., Inc., 1954.

Music in Our Town, Book 2. New York: Silver Burdett Co., 1956.

New Hope for the Retarded. Morris P. and Miriam Pollock. Boston: Porter Sargent, 1953.

Say It and Play It, Action Plays for Children. Edith M. Leonard. White Plains, N. Y.: Row Peterson & Co.

Songs to Grow On. Beatrice Landeck. St. Louis: William Morrow and Co., Inc., 1954.

Speech for the Retarded Child—A Teacher's Handbook, Curriculum Bulletin, 1958-59, Series No. 7, Board of Education of the City of New York, New York Publication Sales Office, 110 Livingston Street, Brooklyn, N.Y.

Syllabus on a Curriculum for the Retarded Child. Staff of PARC Training School, Philadelphia County Chapter, Pennsylvania Association for Retarded Children.

Talking Time. Louise Binder Scott and J. J. Thompson. St. Louis: Webster Publishing Co.

Teach Me. Minnesota Dept. of Public Welfare, 117 University Ave., St. Paul, Minnesota, 1945.

Three R's for the Retarded, The. Naomi H. Chamberlain and Dorothy H. Moss. New York: National Association for Retarded Children.

Wonder Book of Finger Plays and Action Rhymes, The. No. 627 Wonder Books.

II. Books and pamphlets that will provide a background of knowledge and understanding of the problems of mental retardation.

Backward Child, The. (Home training manual published by Canada Dept. of National Health and Welfare.) New York: National Association for Retarded Children.

Curriculum Adjustments for the Mentally Retarded. Elise M. Martens. Bulletin 1950, No. 2, reprint 1953. U.S. Government Printing Office, Washington 25, D.C.

Early Education of the Mentally Retarded. Samuel A. Kirk. Urbana, Illinois: University of Illinois Press, 1958.

Educating the Retarded Child. Samuel Kirk and O. Johnson. Boston: Houghton Mifflin, 1951.

Education of Mentally Handicapped Children. J. E. W. Wallin. New York: Harper and Brothers, 1955.

Education of the Slow-Learning Child. Christine Ingram. New York: The Ronald Press Company, 1953.

Forward Look—The Severely Retarded Child Goes to School, The Arthur S. Hill. Bulletin 1952, No. 11, U.S. Government Printing Office, Washington 25, D.C.

Montesorri Method, The. Maria Montessori translated from the Italian by Anne E. George. Frederick A. Stokes Co.

Other Child: The Brain-Injured Child, The. Richard S. Lewis, and others. New York: Grune and Stratton.

Psychological Problems in Mental Deficiency. Seymour B. Sarason. New York: Harper and Brothers, 1953.

You and Your Retarded Child. S. A. Kirk, M. B. Karnes, and W. D. Kirk. New York: The Macmillan Company, 1955.

Your Child's Speech. (A Practical Guide for Parents for the First Five Years.) Flora Rheta Schreiber. New York: G. P. Putman's Sons.

INDEX

221